DATE DUE

			PRINTED IN U.S.A.

MODERN DRAMATISTS

Modern Dramatists

Series Editors: *Bruce King and Adele King*

Published Titles

Roger Boxill: *Tennessee Williams*
Dennis Carroll: *David Mamet*
Frances Gray: *Noel Coward*
Charles Hayter: *Gilbert and Sullivan*
Gerry McCarthy: *Edward Albee*
Ronald Speirs: *Bertolt Brecht*

Further titles in preparation

MODERN DRAMATISTS

GILBERT AND SULLIVAN

Charles Hayter

St. Martin's Press   New York

First published in the United States of America in 1987

Printed in Hong Kong.

ISBN 0–312–00446–X

Library of Congress Cataloging-in-Publication Data
Hayter, Charles.
Gilbert and Sullivan.
(Modern dramatists)
Bibliography: p.
Includes index.
1. Sullivan, Arthur, Sir, 1842–1900. Operas.
2. Opera. 3. Gilbert, W. S. (William Schwenck),
1836–1911—Criticism and interpretation. I. Title.
II. Series.
ML410.S95H4   1987   782.81′092′2   86–29661
ISBN 0–312–00446–X

Contents

List of Plates

List of Plates

Plates, 3, 4, 7 and 15 are reproduced by kind permission of the Illustrated London News Picture Library. Plates 5, 6, 10, 11, 13 and 14 by kind permission of the Roy Mander and Joe Hitchenson Theatre Collection. Plates 8, 9, are photographs by David Cooper, plates 12, 16 photographs all by Robert Ragsdale, by courtesy of The Stratford Festival, Canada.

Editors' Preface

The *Modern Dramatists* is an international series of introductions to major and significant nineteenth- and twentieth-century dramatists, movements and new forms of drama in Europe, Great Britain, America and new nations such as Nigeria and Trinidad. Besides new studies of great and influential dramatists of the past, the series includes volumes on contemporary authors, recent trends in the theatre and on many dramatists, such as writers of farce, who have created theatre 'classics' while being neglected by literary criticism. The volumes in the series devoted to individual dramatists include a biography, a survey of the plays, and detailed analysis of the most significant plays, along with discussion, where relevant, of the political, social, historical and theatrical context. The authors of the volumes, who are involved with theatre as playwrights, directors, actors, teachers and critics, are concerned with the plays as theatre and discuss such matters as performance, character interpretation and staging, along with themes and contexts.

BRUCE KING
ADELE KING

Preface

Books on nineteenth-century theatre tend to ignore
Gilbert and Sullivan; books on Gilbert and Sullivan tend
to ignore nineteenth-century theatre. This book attempts
to correct this mutual ignorance by looking at the Savoy
Operas from the point of view of their theatrical and
cultural background. The text of the operas used
throughout is the 1962 Oxford University Press edition
by Derek Hudson, which was based on prompt-books
and libretti in the possession of the D'Oyly Carte
Company.

I wish to thank Michael Walters for the initial stimulus
to write this book. I also owe thanks to Harry Benford,
Terence Rees and Jane Yealland for help along the way.

My major debt of gratitude is to my wife Marjorie for
having put up with an absent-minded and absent-bodied
husband during the months of preparation of the
manuscript.

Kingston, Ontario, Canada   CHARLES HAYTER

The Gilbert and Sullivan Operas

Date	Title	Act: Setting	Date of Action
1871	Thespis, or The Gods Grown Old	I: Ruined Temple on the Summit of Olympus II: The same Scene, with Ruins Restored	Classical
1875	Trial by Jury	A Court of Justice	1875
1877	The Sorcerer	I: Exterior of Sir Marmaduke's Mansion, Day II: Same, Night	1877
1878	H.M.S. Pinafore, or The Lass that Loved a Sailor	I: Quarter-Deck of H.M.S. Pinafore, Noon II: Same, Night	1878
1879	The Pirates of Penzance, or The Slave of Duty	I: A Rocky Sea-Shore on the Coast of Cornwall II: A Ruined Chapel by Moonlight	1879
1881	Patience, or Bunthorne's Bride	I: Exterior of Castle Bunthorne II: A Glade	1881
1882	Iolanthe, or The Peer and the Peri	I: An Arcadian Landscape II: Palace Yard, Westminster	1882
1884	Princess Ida, or Castle Adamant	I: Pavilion in King Hildebrand's Palace II: Gardens of Castle Adamant III: Courtyard of Castle Adamant	?
1885	The Mikado, or The Town of Titipu	I: Courtyard of Ko-Ko's Official Residence II: Ko-Ko's Garden	?

Date	Title	Act	Setting	Date of Action
1887	*Ruddigore, or The Witch's Curse*	I:	The Fishing Village of Rederring, Cornwall	Early in the nineteenth century
		II:	Picture Gallery in Ruddigore Castle	
1888	*The Yeomen of the Guard, or The Merryman and his Maid*	I:	Tower Green	Sixteenth century
		II:	The same, moonlight	
1889	*The Gondoliers, or The King of Barataria*	I:	The Piazzetta, Venice	1750
		II:	Pavilion in the Palace of Barataria	
1893	*Utopia Limited, or The Flowers of Progress*	I:	A Utopian Palm Grove	1893
		II:	Throne Room in King Paramount's Palace	
1896	*The Grand Duke, or The Statutory Duel*	I:	Public Square of Speisesaal	1750
		II:	Hall in the Grand Ducal Palace	

1
Overture: the Collaboration

The D'Oyly Carte Opera Company gave the last performance of its 107-year history on 27 February 1982. This company, created in 1875 for the sole purpose of performing the comic operas of W. S. Gilbert and Arthur Sullivan, had survived long past the age at which other relics of Victorian England – even the empire itself – had expired. Its collapse, brought about by the financial difficulties of touring a large repertoire of musical works, broke a direct cultural link with the past century. Although the D'Oyly Carte Company disappeared, the works to which it had devoted itself showed no signs of failing in popularity. In fact, the early years of the 1980s can be said to have marked a renaissance of Gilbert and Sullivan. The most outstanding success was that of *The Pirates of Penzance* on Broadway in a production unfaithful to Sullivan's musical style but strictly faithful to Gilbert's story and words. The Stratford (Ontario) Shakespearean Festival presented its production of *The Mikado* at the reopening of the Old Vic in London, and its choreographic style showed a new approach to movement in the operas. In the United States, the Public Broadcasting Service began broadcasting televised versions of all the operas, including such relatively unfamiliar ones as *Princess Ida* and *Ruddigore* (with movie actor Vincent Price as Sir Despard Murgatroyd). That producers were willing to invest money and artistic energy in these works, for so long regarded as the province of 'terrified amateurs', meant that they were no longer being regarded as quaint mementos of another era but rather as classics with a value of their own.

The value of the Gilbert and Sullivan operas is difficult to describe, for like all dramatic works they are only fully appreciated in performance. To an audience, they mean pleasure; pleasure in listening to words and music exquisitely fitted together; pleasure in delicious word-play and rhymes; pleasure in watching humorous characters extricating themselves from farcical situations. There is also the recognition of universal human weaknesses and pretensions exposed through satire. From a performer's point of view, the operas are exercises in nuance and subtlety, a fact often forgotten by those who would treat them as opera *per se*. The challenge in performing them is the difficulty in adopting the restraint necessary to make the delicate ironies of the dialogue and songs believable. Like the plays of Shakespeare, the operas stretch the performer's awareness of the English language.

The Gilbert and Sullivan operas have a special significance in the history of the British theatre. They are the only works written during the period from 1800 to 1890 that are still performed with any regularity today. Through them, we glimpse the theatre of the mid- and late-nineteenth century. The facetious tone of the operas is borrowed from the Victorian burlesque, their comic devices from the well-made play tradition of melodrama and farce, and their musical structure from the English romantic opera. The operas also contain the seeds of future developments in English drama. Their social comment prepared the way for Shaw, their wit for Wilde, and their nonsensical spirit has more than a trace of absurdism. Furthermore, the original productions of the operas reflected the important advances in stage management, direction and design being made in this period, and indeed Gilbert's methods as a director had a great influence on all who came in touch with him. His insistence on truthfulness and restraint in comic acting marked a clear departure from the bombastic, oratorical acting style of the early part of the century.

William Schwenck Gilbert (1836–1911), comic poet and librettist, had, like many eminent Victorians, a dual personality. His life was that of a respectable middle-class gentleman: born the son of a naval surgeon, he was educated at the University of London and, following a brief career in the civil service, entered the legal profession. Whether it was as a private citizen suing others, or as (in later life) a crusty Justice of the Peace, the law was one of Gilbert's main preoccupations throughout his life. Almost every Gilbert and Sullivan opera contains some character or reference to the legal profession, whether it is *Trial by Jury* which is from start to finish a burlesque of courtroom drama, or Sir Bailey Barre in *Utopia, Ltd.*:

A complicated gentleman allow me to present,
Of all the arts and faculties the terse embodiment,
He's a great Arithmetician who can demonstrate with
  ease

3

That two and two are three, or five, or anything you
  please;
An eminent Logician who can make it clear to you
That black is white – when looked at from the proper
  point of view;
A marvellous Philologist who'll undertake to show
That 'yes' is but another and a neater form of 'no'.

Many of the plots turn on points of interpretation of
fictional laws. Here is the denouement of *Iolanthe*:

> FAIRY QUEEN: You have all incurred death; but I can't
> slaughter the whole company! And yet (*unfolding a
> scroll*) the law is clear – every fairy must die who
> marries a mortal!
>
> LORD CHANCELLOR: Allow me, as an old equity
> draughtsman, to make a suggestion. The subtleties
> of the legal mind are equal to the emergency. The
> thing is really quite simple – the insertion of a single
> word will do it. Let it stand that every fairy shall die
> who don't marry a mortal, and there you are, out of
> your difficulty at once!

There is an echo of the courtroom in much of the
dialogue in the Savoy Operas, in which characters wrangle
over interpretations of events as skilfully – and often as
tediously – as lawyers. At the opening of Act II of *The
Gondoliers*, there occurs the following interchange
between Marco and Giuseppe and their household:

> GIUSEPPE: It is arranged that, until it is decided which
> of us two is the actual King, we are to act as one
> person.
>
> GIORGIO: Exactly.

GIUSEPPE: Now, although we act as one person, we are, in point of fact, two persons.

ANNIBALE: Ah, I don't think we can go into that. It is a legal fiction, and legal fictions are solemn things. Situated as we are, we can't recognise two independent responsibilities.

GIUSEPPE: No; but you can recognise two independent appetites. It's all very well to say we act as one person, but when you supply us with only one ration between us, I should describe it as a legal fiction carried a little too far.

ANNIBALE: It's rather a nice point. I don't like to express an opinion off-hand. Suppose we reserve it for argument before the full Court?

MARCO: Yes, but what are we to do in the meantime?

MARCO and GIUSEPPE: We want our tea.

ANNIBALE: I think we may make an interim order for double rations on their Majesties entering into the usual undertaking to indemnify in the event of an adverse decision?

GIORGIO: That, I think, will meet the case. But you must work hard – stick to it – nothing like work.

The nineteenth century was a period of rapid change in British society. In every area of life, old values were threatened and replaced by new ideas. Scientific advancements were demolishing the traditional doctrines of religion and philosophy; industrialisation was changing the nature and pattern of human labour; and technology was transforming the environment into the modern urban landscape. The forces of change are seen in Gilbert's play *Sweethearts* (1874). The first act, set in 1844, takes place in the garden of a country villa where open country is seen in the distance. The second act takes place thirty years later, and 'the landscape has . . . undergone a metamorphosis, inasmuch as that which was open country in Act I is now covered with picturesque semi-detached villas, and there are indications of a large town in the distance.' In such a world of change, government attempted to impose order through an ever-increasing number of acts and regulations governing all areas of human life from sanitation to education. Gilbert's preoccupation with law reflects this intrusion of the state into the life of the individual. He shares this theme with other Victorian writers, most notably Dickens, who viewed Britain's legal institutions as hopelessly corrupt and inhumane. Perhaps because he was a lawyer himself, Gilbert's view was more merciful. Dickens' vision of the Court of Chancery in *Bleak House* is grim, but Gilbert's portrait of the same institution in *Iolanthe* is relieved by humour:

> The law is the true embodiment
> Of everything that's excellent.
> It has no kind of fault or flaw,
> And I, my Lords, embody the Law.
> The constitutional guardian I
> Of pretty young wards in Chancery,
> All very agreeable girls – and none
> Are over the age of twenty-one.

One consequence of the pressures of living in an age of rapid social and political change was the retreat of many Victorians into imaginative worlds of nonsense and fantasy. Lewis Carroll (1832–98) is the best known example of a Victorian double life: he was both the Reverend Charles Lutwidge Dodgson, Lecturer in Mathematics, and Lewis Carroll, author of 'The Hunting of the Snark' and *Through the Looking-Glass*. In a similar way, Gilbert's respectable public life hid the eccentricities and oddities of his imagination. An early expression of his nonsense streak occurred in the 1860s when, under the pen-name 'Bab', he wrote and illustrated nonsense poems for the magazine *Fun*. A common theme of these poems – known as the *Bab Ballads* – is the tension between conformity and individuality. Characters behave in ways that are at odds with their prescribed roles in society:

> Policeman Peter Forth I drag
> From his obscure retreat:
> He was a merry, genial wag,
> Who loved a mad conceit.
> If he were asked the time of day
> By country bumpkins green,
> He not unfrequently would say,
> 'A quarter past thirteen.'
>
> If ever you by word of mouth
> Inquired of Mister Forth
> The way to somewhere in the South,
> He always sent you North.
> With little boys his beat along
> He loved to stop and play;
> He loved to send old ladies wrong,
> And teach their feet to stray.

Many such characters foreshadow those in the operas. For example, Captain Reece is the prototype of Captain Corcoran in *H.M.S. Pinafore*:

> Of all the ships upon the blue,
> No ship contained a better crew
> Than that of worthy Captain Reece,
> Commanding of the Mantelpiece.

7

> He was adored by all his men,
> For worthy Captain Reece, R.N.,
> Did all that lay within him to
> Promote the comfort of his crew.
> If ever they were dull or sad
> Their captain danced to them like mad,
> Or told, to make the time pass by,
> Droll legends of his infancy.
> A feather bed had every man,
> Warm slippers and hot-water can,
> Brown windsor from the captain's store,
> A valet too, to every four.

In these poems, Gilbert began to sharpen the satiric darts that fill the operas. Favourite objects of his satire include military men:

> General John was a soldier tried,
> A chief of warlike dons;
> A haughty stride and a withering pride
> Were Major-General John's.

and clergymen:

> The Reverend Micah Sowls,
> He shouts and yells and howls,
> He screams, he mouths, he bumps,
> He foams, he rants, he thumps.

As in the operas, the humour is mixed with the macabre. In 'The Yarn of the Nancy Bell', the chief character is a sailor who has eaten his fellow crew members in order to survive a shipwreck, and in 'Annie Protheroe', the title character's boyfriend is a 'gentle executioner':

And when his work was over, they would ramble o'er
  the lea,
And sit beneath the frondage of an elderberry tree.
And Annie's simple prattle entertained him on his
  walk,
For public executions formed the subject of her talk,
And sometimes he'd explain to her, which charmed
  her very much,
How famous operators vary very much in touch,
And then, perhaps, he'd show how he himself
  performed the trick,
And illustrate his meaning with a poppy and a stick.

This passage demonstrates the nimbleness with rhyme and rhythm which is seen in the songs of the operas.

While he was gaining popularity as a comic poet, Gilbert began to develop his talents as a dramatist. At the age of 18 he had written a burlesque which had been unsuccessfully offered to 'every manager in London', but it was not until the production in 1866 of *Dulcamara, or, The Little Duck and the Great Quack*, a burlesque of Donizetti's *L'Elisir D'Amore*, that he achieved recognition. During the next decade, until the appearance of *The Sorcerer* in 1877, Gilbert wrote and had produced almost fifty works for the stage. He worked in all the popular Victorian dramatic forms: melodrama (*Dan'l Druce*, 1876); burlesque (*The Merry Zingara*, 1868); pantomime (*Harlequin Cock-Robin*, 1867); comedy (*On Guard*, 1869); farce (*Allow Me To Explain*, 1867); and comic opera (*Princess Toto*, 1876). The vast majority of these works are undistinguished and reflect the mediocrity of mid-Victorian playwriting. *On Guard*, for example, is a conventional Victorian comedy in that it is not a comedy at all but a melodrama with weakly humorous incidents.

In several of his early plays, however, Gilbert strained against the conventions of Victorian drama and occasionally produced works of unusual interest. Among these are the comic plays he wrote in the 1860s for the Royal Gallery of Illustration and the two prose comedies *Tom Cobb* (1875) and *Engaged* (1877). In the latter plays, instead of taking the conventions of melodrama seriously, he treats them with whimsical parody. In *Tom Cobb*, the coincidences which form the main basis for the plots of melodrama are satirised when Tom says:

> Well, well – there is a grim justice in the
> fact that my punishment will be brought about
> through the employers of the son of the
> husband of the mother of the young woman to
> whom I was to have been married.

In *Engaged*, there is continual ridiculing of melodramatic threats:

> BELVAWNEY: If any girl has succeeded in enslaving you – and I know how easily you are enslaved – dismiss her from your thoughts; have no more to say to her; and I will – yes, I will bless you with my latest breath!
> CHEVIOT: Whether a blessing conferred with one's latest breath is a superior article to one conferred in robust health we need not stop to inquire.

Such theatrical burlesque is found throughout the operas. In *Topsyturvydom*, an 'original extravaganza' presented in 1874, there is a blend of fantasy and satire identical to that of the Bab Ballads and the operas. It concerns the visit of Mr Satis, MP, to the kingdom of Imiprimus the Inverted, where everything is the opposite of the way it should be. Ceilings are floors, people grow younger instead of older, they wipe their heads on doormats and their feet on handkerchiefs, and the monarch thrills at being reviled by his people. The National Anthem is an inverted parody of 'God Save The Queen'.

> Fiends dissect our Royal Master,
> Tear asunder limb from limb.
> May all kinds of black disaster
> Now accumulate for him.

The piece is full of political jibes, as when the king says, 'Our Parliament is composed of wealthy donkeys who are elected partly because they are wealthy and partly because they are donkeys.'

Other early works by Gilbert contain satire of a more general nature, as in the blank-verse play *The Palace of Truth* (1870) where it is impossible to live in a place where each person must speak the truth. The characters' inability to carry on without the cloaks of pretension and hypocrisy demonstrates Gilbert's cynicism, which surfaces sometimes in the operas. In another poetic comedy, *The Wicked World* (1873), Gilbert demonstrates the corrupting power of love. Shocked by the ever-increasing wickedness of the world, fairies summon two men to fairyland to show them how they can better conduct their lives. Ironically, the fairies fall in love with the two men, and the ensuing jealousies and rivalries destroy the bliss of fairyland. Love is depicted as the root of all earthly evils:

Why Love's the germ
Of every sin that stalks upon the earth:
The brawler fights for love – the drunkard drinks
To toast the girl who loves him, or to drown
Remembrance of the girl who loves him not!
The miser hoards his gold to purchase love.
The liar lies to gain, or wealth, or love;
And if for wealth, it is to purchase love.
The very footpad nerves his coward arm
To stealthy deeds of shame by pondering on
The tipsy kisses of some tavern wench!
Be not deceived – this love is but the seed;
The branching tree that springs from it is
Hate!

This proved too much for Victorian audiences, and Gilbert became embroiled in one of his perennial lawsuits with the *Pall Mall Gazette* which labelled the play vulgar, coarse and indecent. Gilbert won the suit, and in doing so vindicated his place as the angry young man of the 1860s theatre. Probably the high point of this phase of his career came when the eminent critic Joseph Knight disparagingly compared Gilbert to Ibsen, whose works were at that point just filtering through to a disapproving Britain.

If Gilbert was branded as an iconoclast, Arthur Seymour Sullivan (1842–1900) was the darling of late-Victorian society. While Sullivan received his knighthood in 1883, Gilbert had to wait until 1907. Sullivan's rise to the forefront of late-Victorian composers was effortless. He was born into a musical family, his father being sergeant bandmaster at the Royal Military College, Sandhurst. Echoes of the martial music to which Sullivan was constantly exposed as a boy run throughout his later work, as in the first act of *Patience*:

> The soldiers of our Queen
> Are linked in friendly tether;
> Upon the battle scene
> They fight the foe together . . .

At the age of ten he was chosen to become one of the select group of Choristers of Her Majesty's Chapel Royal. Four years later he won the first Mendelssohn Scholarship to study at the Royal Academy of Music, and from 1858 to 1861 he completed his musical education studying under masters in Leipzig. The excellence of his musical training had a dual effect on Sullivan's later career. It meant that the music for his comic operas was of the highest quality both in terms of content and craftsmanship; this has had no small part in the endurance of the Savoy Operas. On the other hand, on his return from Europe Sullivan was hailed as the bright young hope of English music, the man who would restore it to greatness. When his music for Shakespeare's *The Tempest* was performed at the Crystal Palace in 1862, one reviewer said:

> It was one of those events which mark an epoch in a man's life; and, what is of more universal consequence, it may mark an epoch in English music, or we shall be greatly disappointed. Years on years have elapsed since we have heard a work by so young an artist so full of promise, so full of fancy, showing so much conscientiousness, so much skill, and so few references to any model elect.[1]

Throughout the rest of his life, Sullivan was forced to wear the yoke of great expectations. He produced much serious music, including hymns ('Onward, Christian Soldiers'), oratorios (*The Light of the World*, 1873), and symphonies (*Irish Symphony*, 1866), and he was in great demand as a conductor at music festivals. His efforts as a serious composer, though, were a source of continual disappointment to those who expected greatness of him, and none of his serious works has earned a place in the modern musical repertoire. Even in the field of opera, Sullivan's one attempt at grand opera, *Ivanhoe* (1891), had to be withdrawn before it could recoup its costs.

Sullivan's failure as a serious musician has been ascribed to his indolence and love of pleasure:

> Compare Sullivan with Brahms. Of the two I think Sullivan had the greater natural musical talent; but Brahms will not write a note he doesn't think worthy of his gift. . . . As for Sullivan, he settles in London, and writes and publishes things quite unworthy of his genius. He is petted by Royalty, mixes in aristocratic circles, acquires expensive tastes which oblige him to prostitute his talents for money-making works. As a consequence, his modes of expression deteriorate, and England and the world are robbed of the fruit of his God-given gifts.[2]

But a case could also be made that Sullivan's natural 'God-given' talents did not lie in the direction of serious music at all but in the field of comic music. His skills in light opera first became evident in 1866 when he composed the music for *Cox and Box*, F. C. Burnand's light operatic version of one of the most popular Victorian farces, *Box and Cox*. The following year, he wrote a two-act comic opera (again with Burnand as librettist) called

The Contrabandista, and in 1875 a 'musical folly' called *The Zoo*, set at the London Zoo.

While most of the standard histories of the collaboration emphasise the differences between librettist and composer, in the use of comedy as the medium for his imagination Sullivan was akin to Gilbert. Outside as well as inside the theatre, both men were wits and shared a similar comic view of life. Sullivan's scores are as witty as any of Gilbert's words or characters. Much as *Princess Ida* demonstrates Sullivan's serious yearnings, it also shows him at his cleverest, as in the music he wrote for the entrance of King Gama's three sons, where the deliberate stodginess of the music expresses their cloddishness:

> We are warriors three,
> Sons of Gama, Rex,
> Like most sons are we,
> Masculine in sex.

For both men, attempts to write in a serious way seemed stilted and unnatural. Gilbert, like Sullivan, attempted to establish a reputation for himself as a serious artist, but unlike his partner recognised early on the futility of doing so. This realisation only came to Sullivan late in his career when, plagued with illness, his artistic powers were diminished. There is a touching story told about him watching a performance of *Ivanhoe* with obvious dissatisfaction and turning to his companion to say 'a cobbler should stick to his last'.

The partnership of W. S. Gilbert and Arthur Sullivan began in 1871 with *Thespis, or The Gods Grown Old*. John Hollingshead, the manager of the Gaiety Theatre, had already made use of Gilbert's talents as a dramatist, and for the Christmas season of 1871 he asked Sullivan to compose music for a new piece by Gilbert. The result was an 'entirely original grotesque Opera in two acts' which followed in the tradition of the classical burlesque established by James Robinson Planché some thirty years earlier. Despite its success, *Thespis* was never revived (and is not likely to be so now because the original music is lost). Librettist and composer took divergent paths until 1875 when Richard D'Oyly Carte brought them together to write the one-act 'dramatic cantata', *Trial by Jury*. At that time, D'Oyly Carte was manager of the Royalty Theatre, and he commissioned the piece as a curtain-raiser to Offenbach's *La Périchole*. It was partly as a reaction to the popularity of the French *opéra bouffe* that D'Oyly Carte determined to keep the librettist and composer together, for he saw in them the means of establishing an English school of light opera. In 1874 he proclaimed: 'It is my desire to establish in London a permanent abode for light opera, played with all the completeness and attention to detail which is recognised in the representations given at even mediocre Continental theatres.'

In 1876, D'Oyly Carte's idea came to fruition, for he obtained enough financial backing to establish a Comedy Opera Company and lease the Opera Comique Theatre. It was here that the first major successes of Gilbert and Sullivan, *The Sorcerer* (1877) and *H.M.S. Pinafore, or The Lass that Loved a Sailor* (1878) were performed. The first, billed as a 'New and Original Modern Comic Opera', was based on the love-potion theme of *L'Elisir d'Amore* which Gilbert had already burlesqued in *Dulcamara*; the second, 'an entirely Original Nautical Opera', followed in the tradition of nautical drama so well established in the nineteenth century. The success of these operas was based not only on the quality of the writing but on the excellence of production, for D'Oyly Carte gave Gilbert and Sullivan a free hand in matters of casting, rehearsal, design and direction. Gilbert in particular exercised an artistic control over the productions that unified them in a way unusual in the theatrical practice of the day. To ensure authenticity in the sets and costumes for *Pinafore*, for example, he travelled to Portsmouth to make sketches of ships and sailors. In rehearsal, he carefully supervised the exact manner of delivery of dialogue and each gesture and posture of movement.

By 1879 the Comedy Opera Company had dissolved and Gilbert, Sullivan and D'Oyly Carte entered into a business partnership by which the profits from the comic operas would be divided equally among them. During this period there was no international copyright law, so that English works were frequently seen in unauthorised or 'pirated' versions on the American stage. Such was its popularity on the western side of the Atlantic that at one time there were eight pirated versions of *Pinafore* running simultaneously in New York for which the authors received not one cent. In order to subvert the pirates the partners decided to present the premiere of their next opera in New York, and so *The Pirates of Penzance, or The Slave of Duty* opened at the Fifth Avenue Theatre on 31 December 1879. It was first seen at the Opera Comique in London in the spring of 1880. This 'New and Original Melodramatic Opera' ran for a year, and was replaced in April of 1881 by *Patience, or Bunthorne's Bride*, an 'Aesthetic Opera' which satirised the aesthetic movement in art and decoration.

The enormous financial success of these operas enabled D'Oyly Carte to build a theatre devoted expressly to their presentation. This was the Savoy, still in use today, and whose name was given to the works of Gilbert and Sullivan ('Savoy Operas') and to the performers of them ('Savoyards'). This was the first theatre in the world to be lit entirely by electricity, and when *Iolanthe, or The Peer and the Peri* appeared in 1882 the head-dresses and wands of the fairies were illuminated by electric lights. In 1884 came *Princess Ida, or Castle Adamant*, which was based on Gilbert's burlesque of Tennyson's poem 'The Princess'. It differed in several ways from the previous operas: it was written in three acts, with dialogue written in blank verse, and required a considerably larger cast of characters. But its satire (of higher education for women, hardly a laughing matter today) linked it in spirit with its predecessors.

Following *Princess Ida* the first serious artistic conflict between librettist and composer occurred. Sullivan suddenly declared he would compose no more comic operas; he felt that his musical style was becoming repetitious and he was frustrated with the secondary role of the music in the operas:

> I will be quite frank. With Princess Ida I have come to the end of my tether – the end of my capability in that class of piece. My tunes are in danger of becoming mere repetitions of my former pieces, my concerted movements are getting to possess a strong family likeness and I have rung all the changes possible in the way of variety of rhythm. It has hitherto been word-setting, I might almost say syllable-setting, for I have looked upon the words as being of such importance that I have been continually keeping down the music in order that not one should be lost.[3]

He also objected to what he termed the 'unreality' of Gilbert's stories. The last complaint appeared to be confirmed when Gilbert presented him with a proposal for the plot of the next opera, which was to concern a magic lozenge by which people could turn into their opposites. After a month's heated correspondence, Gilbert withdrew the lozenge plot and substituted the topic and story which on 14 March 1885 appeared as *The Mikado, or The Town of Titipu*. Although this work was born out of the first serious disagreement between the collaborators, it held the stage of the Savoy for longer than any of its predecessors.

In 1887 came *Ruddigore, or The Witch's Curse*, a 'Supernatural Opera' in which the pair returned to the mode of theatrical burlesque and this time mocked the characters and conventions of 'blood and thunder' melodrama. *The Yeomen of the Guard, or The Merryman and his Maid*, which followed in 1889, was a clear departure from the previous series in its serious tone which placed it on a level between comic and grand opera. Despite its more realistic story, lack of burlesque, and opportunity for grander music, Sullivan was still dissatisfied and again threatened to withdraw from the partnership, citing once more the 'improbability' of Gilbert's plots:

I have lost the liking for writing comic opera, and entertain very grave doubts as to my power of doing it. You yourself have reproached me directly and indirectly with the seriousness of my music, fitted more for the cathedral than the comic opera stage, and I cannot but feel that in very many cases the reproach is just. I have lost the necessary nerve for it, and it is not too much to say that it is distasteful to me. The types used over and over again (unavoidable in such a company as ours), the Grossmith part, the middle-aged woman with fading charms, cannot again be clothed with music by me. Nor can I again write to any wildly improbable plot in which there is not some human interest.

Beneath these objections lay Sullivan's ambition to write a serious opera. This conflict was resolved when plans were fixed for him to write a grand opera with Julian Sturgis as librettist (this subsequently appeared as *Ivanhoe*). With his serious ambitions about to be fulfilled, Sullivan agreed to another comic opera with Gilbert; the result was *The Gondoliers, or The King of Barataria*, which had its première in December 1889.

The following year brought the Carpet Quarrel, in which Gilbert took issue with D'Oyly Carte about the cost of some new carpets for the Savoy. Gilbert's argument was not with Sullivan, but he felt that the composer was on D'Oyly Carte's side, and the famous team ended up glaring at each other from opposite sides of a courtroom. The acrimony expressed in this quarrel was too much for the partnership to bear, and on 5 May 1890 Gilbert wrote to Sullivan declaring that 'the time for putting an end to our collaboration has at last arrived'.

Following this break, they largely went separate ways. Although Sullivan wrote music for other librettists (*Haddon Hall*, 1891) and Gilbert libretti for other composers (*The Mountebanks*, 1892, in which at long last he used his cherished lozenge plot), these works did not achieve the success of their joint accomplishments. They were reunited twice in the 1890s, first for the lavish *Utopia Ltd., or The Flowers of Progress* (1893), and the feeble *The Grand Duke, or The Statutory Duel* in 1896. Sullivan died in 1900, and Gilbert retreated to a country estate where he spent the rest of his life as an Edwardian country gentleman, raising exotic animals and toying with photography and automobiles.

The traditional view of the relationship between the two men is that Gilbert exercised complete authority over Sullivan and that it was the latter's unhappiness with his subservience that led to the break-up of the partnership. Sullivan's letters to Gilbert and D'Oyly Carte in which he complains about the secondary role of the music would appear to support this view. But in actual fact there was much more give and take between composer and librettist than is usually thought. The topic for at least one of the operas, *The Gondoliers*, was suggested by Sullivan, and throughout the preparation of each libretto the composer played an important role in modifying Gilbert's ideas. In 1894 Gilbert gave an interview in which he described their creative method:

'Oh', said Mr. Gilbert, 'I suppose we do it pretty much as any other two persons would who collaborate. In the first place, we arrange a meeting and I propose a subject, which, if entertained at all, is freely and fully discussed in all its bearings. Assuming that the broader lines of the plot have been thus settled, I write a scenario of fairish length – say twenty-six to thirty pages of foolscap – and this is subjected in its turn to a fresh discussion, and as a consequence, a second, third, or even fourth version of the scenario may be rendered necessary. Those passages and situations Sir Arthur thinks unsuitable to musical treatment I either modify or perhaps eliminate altogether. If I find that his difficulties or objections in any way knock the keystone out of my plan I tell him so, and he in turn yields a point or two.

By this mode of procedure it will be readily perceived

that there is some degree of give and take. Before a final plan is decided upon, we may meet several times and gradually remove such obstacles as are likely to cause any hitch in the future harmonious blending of the dialogue and music.'[4]

That Sullivan did indeed have influence on the libretti is confirmed by passages from his diary during the writing of *The Mikado*, when he states that after Gilbert showed him the first act he 'made several important suggestions with which Gilbert agreed'. Often forgotten is that after the 1884 quarrel it was Gilbert who gave way, dropping the lozenge plot in favour of the farcical but somewhat more realistic elements of *The Mikado*. The difference between the early and late Savoy operas consists in changes in Gilbert's style made to accommodate Sullivan's wishes. The composer's complaint that the music did not play a large enough role was met by the inclusion of musical numbers of greater length and complexity, to the point where the first forty-five minutes of *The Gondoliers* is uninterrupted music. His distaste for 'unreality' in plot and character was met by a gradual downplaying of burlesque and satire in the libretti and a greater emphasis on romance and light-hearted whimsy. In fact, the main source of Gilbert's development as a dramatist during his Savoy years was the influence of his composer.

2
Curtain-Raiser: the Theatrical Background

On 29 March 1869, Priscilla and Thomas German Reed, proprietors of the Royal Gallery of Illustration, presented on the same bill *Cox and Box*, a 'triumviretta' with words by F. C. Burnand and music by Arthur Sullivan, and *No Cards*, a musical piece in one act with words by W. S. Gilbert. Sullivan had already composed a two-act comic opera titled *The Contrabandista* for the Reeds, and *No Cards* was the first of several successful pieces Gilbert was to write for the Gallery of Illustration. Although Gilbert and Sullivan never produced a joint work for them, the Reeds have rightfully been called 'the godparents of the Savoy Operas'.[1]

Like the Bancrofts at the Prince of Wales Theatre, the Reeds sought to improve the artistic standards of the Victorian theatre. In the early nineteenth century, the rise in London of a large, uneducated working-class audience had driven the middle and upper classes from the theatres. The playhouses, in the age of Sheridan the homes of fashion and society, 'succumbed to the rabble as a weakened constitution might to a virulent disease'.[2] Spectacle replaced spoken drama: at Sadler's Wells Theatre in 1804 the stage was replaced by a tank to accommodate water dramas which featured miniature navies engaging in sea battles. The successful playwrights were no longer the bright literary talents of the day but hacks who gave the audiences easy laughter and tears, strong moral and patriotic sentiment, and thrilling spectacle. As the fare at most theatres declined, so did the physical conditions: Dickens described the conspicuous 'presence of dirt, and absence of paint' in the early Victorian playhouse. By 1868, theatrical conditions deteriorated to the point where one observer remarked: 'We are justified in concluding that the drama has reached a lower stage in its decline that at any former period of its existence, and that, as a peculiar institution, it closely approximates to utter extinction.'[3]

The dominant theatrical form of the nineteenth century was melodrama. Its general features have been summarised by Ernest Watson:

What we in general mean by melodrama, I take it, is a plot which has little but its mechanics to recommend it, in which characters of impossible and conventional vices and virtues act with a kind of mathematical precision, but insufficient motivation, according to type, and in which, moreover, the most impossible situations are introduced to baulk the heroes, who similarly are extricated from their difficulties by the frankly exposed machinery of the plot, – or, worse, yet, of the stage mechanician.[4]

Curtain-Raiser: the Theatrical Background

The Adelphi Theatre, opened in 1806, was the earliest home of sensational melodrama in London: here murders, tortures, wicked baronets, imprisoned maidens, castles, spectres, goblins and vampires thrilled audiences each night. Melodrama maintained its popularity throughout the century. Its excitement can be appreciated in a scene from a late-nineteenth-century play *The Bells* (1871) by Leopold Lewis, in which a burgomaster is haunted by guilt after murdering a Polish Jew:

MATHIAS: (*alone – comes forward and listens in terror. Music with frequent chords*).
Bells! Bells!
He runs to the window and, slightly drawing the curtains looks out.) No one on the road. What is this jangling in my ears? What is tonight? Ah, it is the very night, the very hour! (*Clock strikes ten.*) I feel a darkness coming over me.
(*Stage darkens*)
A sensation of giddiness seizes me. (*He staggers to chair*) Shall I call for help? No, no Mathias. Have courage! The Jew is dead! (*Sinks on chair; the Bells come closer; then the back of the Scene rises and sinks, disclosing the Bridge of Vechem, with the snow-covered country and frozen rivulet; lime-kiln burning in the distance. The Jew is discovered seated in sledge dressed as described in speech in Act 1; the horse carrying Bells; the Jew's face is turned away. The snow is falling fast; the scene is seen through a gauze; limelight. Vision of a man dressed in a brown blouse and hood over his head, carrying an axe; stands in an attitude of following the sledge. When the picture is fully disclosed the Bells cease.*)
MATHIAS: (*his back to scene*). Oh, it is nothing. It is the

wine and cold that have overcome me! (*He rises and turns; goes up stage; starts violently upon seeing the vision before him. At the same time the Jew in the sledge suddenly turns his face, which is ashy pale, and fixes his eyes sternly upon him. Mathias utters a prolonged cry of terror, and falls senseless. Hurried Music.*)

Judged by literary values alone, this piece is poor, but in terms of theatrical power, the spectacle is as vivid as cinema. Melodrama represents the paradox of mid-nineteenth-century theatre: while the period did not produce any great dramatic literature, it was a time of great vigour and activity in theatrical production. As George Rowell observes in *The Victorian Theatre*:

> No other period in English theatre history illustrates so clearly the fact that a play exists only fully in performance. Many plays of the period, famous in their day, appear scarcely intelligible on the printed page. . . . To recreate from the text a performance of a Victorian play calls for an imagination strongly disciplined to the theatrical practice of the day.

If melodrama flourished, comedy regressed. The English tradition of comedy of manners, in which amusement rested on witty dialogue and social satire, appeared to have died with Sheridan in 1816. Most mid-Victorian comedies are melodramas with comic relief provided by eccentric characters performing amusing stage business. Tom Taylor's *Our American Cousin* (1861) is a good example. The plot concerns the attempts of the hero, Asa Trenchard, to foil plans by the villain to gain control of Sir Edward Trenchard's fortune and marry his daughter Florence. This provides the framework for the introduction of several comic characters, chief of whom is Lord Dundreary. Although he is totally irrelevant to the main action, Dundreary dominates the play in scenes such as this:

FLORENCE: He [Asa] writes from Brattleboro', Vermont, 'Quite well, just come in from a shooting party, with a party of Crows, splendid fellows, six feet high.'

DUNDREARY: Birds six feet high, what tremendous animals they must be.

FLORENCE: Oh, I see what my brother means; a tribe of Indians called Crows, not birds.

DUNDREARY: Oh, I thought you meant those creatures with wings on them.

FLORENCE: Wings?

DUNDREARY: I mean those things that move, breathe and walk, they look like animals with those things. (*Moving his arms like wings.*)

FLORENCE: Wings.

DUNDREARY: Birds with wings, that's the idea.

The thin humour of the dialogue was enlivened by the acting of Edward Sothern, who made the part of Dundreary his own. However deficient the period was in the writing of comedy, it was an age of great comic actors. Like melodrama, the texts of comedy are a shorthand for performance; they are filled with vague stage directions such as 'Business with letter', 'Repeat business', and 'This to be worked up'. Such directions provided opportunity for insertion of bits of slapstick or other gags.

Middle-class Victorians shunned the theatres not only because of the unpleasant surroundings and coarse fare but also because of their own Puritanical attitudes. By the 1870s, there were signs of change. There was increasing recognition of the value of the theatre in the moral education of the public. *The Theatre* of 1 November 1879, has a leading article called 'Regenerating the Stage' which describes a meeting chaired by the Bishop of Manchester where papers such as 'On the Power of the Drama as a Moral Teacher' were heard. Under the guise of moral edification, the middle classes slowly moved back to the theatre. Their attendance was helped by the efforts of managements like the Reeds who made an effort to cater to the respectability of their customers. Their advertisements avoided all sense of impropriety. In much the same way that Victorian tableclothes hid the legs of the tea-table, the Reeds clothed their undertakings in non-theatrical terms: plays were called 'illustrations' and roles 'assumptions'. Although the light pieces that they played bubbled with the Victorian nonsense spirit, they were completely free of any coarseness or vulgarity. Following in the steps of the Bancrofts, the Reeds paid close attention to the comfort of their audiences. In stark contrast to the circus-like atmosphere of early Victorian theatre, the interior of the Gallery of Illustration was as solemn as a chapel. F. C. Burnand described the ushers as 'attendants not very distantly related to pew-openers'.

Burnand's image of theatre as church is significant. It recurs in other descriptions of later Victorian playhouses. Henry James described the replies of a ticket clerk in a London theatre in 1877 as being like liturgical responses in church.[5] This shift of tone represents the new respectability of the theatre in the eyes of the middle classes by the 1870s and 1880s. Through the efforts of the Reeds, the Bancrofts, Irving and others, the middle classes came to enjoy theatre with as much diligent fervour as religion and politics. Gilbert and Sullivan reaped the reward of this preparation. When they began their collaboration, they found a receptive and ready-made audience for their works in the urban middle class who attended the theatre without guilt or embarrassment. It is no surprise to find in a review of *The Gondoliers* on its opening night in 1889 an echo of the atmosphere at the Gallery of Illustration twenty years before:

> The house was crowded, but it seemed to me less like an audience than a congregation. They had heard of Gilbert and Sullivan, and had come to worship at their shrine as they would go on Sunday to sit under Stopford Brooke or Dr. Parker or Mr. Spurgeon. They offered one another one half of their books of the words as good people do when they are put in a strange pew at church.[6]

The enormous influence on the Savoy Operas of the comic works that Gilbert wrote for the Reeds is thoroughly dealt with by Jane Stedman in *Gilbert Before Sullivan*. The Gallery of Illustration provided a laboratory for Gilbert's comic technique, and many of the plots and comic ideas of his subsequent comic operas have their origin in the six pieces he wrote for the Reeds. In *Our Island Home*, Captain Bang, the Pirate King, became a pirate – like Frederic in *The Pirates of Penzance* – because his nurserymaid mistook the word 'pirate' for 'pilot'. Like *Ruddigore*, *Ages Ago* features a portrait gallery that comes to life. *Happy Arcadia* provides lines or ideas which crop up in no less than eight of the Savoy Operas. Among the songs in this piece is an Identity Quartette which starts:

> The question of identity
> Suppose we now discuss.
> It seems that all of us are me
> And neither of us *us*!

This piece prefigures the more famous quartet from *The Gondoliers*, 'In a contemplative fashion'.

The Reeds were not the only godparents of the Savoy Operas. Other influences included Offenbach, whose music had been used to accompany comic pieces at the Gallery of Illustration. A reason for the English theatre's low esteem in the mid-nineteenth century was its complete domination by French dramatic forms. The French critic, Augustin Filon, observed in 1897: 'There was no getting along without us French between 1850 and 1865. We were translated and adapted in every form.'[7] Taking advantage of the lack of an international copyright law, the British theatre pillaged the flourishing French drama for melodramas, farces, comedies, comedy-dramas, comediettas, and a multitude of other hybrid theatrical forms. Shortly after their introduction in Paris the operettas of Jacques Offenbach (1819–80) were ferried across the English Channel. In the 1860s Offenbach, setting music to libretti by Henri Meilhac and Ludovic Halevy, produced a distinct style of light musical work known as *opéra bouffe*. These pieces were constructed on the standard plan of the already well-established *opéra comique* – a humorous story told through spoken dialogue alternating with specially composed music – but included racier dialogue, more pungent satire and generally more shameless frivolity than their predecessors. Offenbach's first major success was *Orpheus in the Underworld* (1858), which parodied the mythological story of Orpheus and Eurydice. Classical parody had a long history on the

French stage, but this piece made the idea seem entirely fresh with its 'gods in carnival costume, scattering jokes and witticisms in the jargon of the Boulevards'[8] and its waltzes, *galops* and naughty cancan. After *Orpheus* came a string of successes: *La Belle Hélène*, also a burlesque of antiquity; *Bluebeard*, a send-up of the legend of the famous pirate; and *La Vie Parisienne*, which satirised the manners of the day. *The Grand Duchess of Gerolstein* contained political and military satire in a lighthearted comedy of intrigue.

Gilbert and Sullivan could not escape the influence of Offenbach. *Orpheus in the Underworld* appeared in English in 1865 and *La Belle Hélène* and *Bluebeard* both appeared in London in the same year as their Paris premieres. Sullivan had seen productions of Offenbach in Paris, and his first essay in comic opera, *Cox and Box*, appeared on the same programme as the Frenchman's *Les Deux Aveuglés*. In 1871, Gilbert had rendered a translation of *Les Brigands*. The second Gilbert and Sullivan collaboration, *Trial by Jury*, was written as an afterpiece to *La Périchole*. It is no accident that Richard D'Oyly Carte chose to place a portrait of Offenbach above those of Gilbert and Sullivan on the front cover of his Royalty Theatre programme.

Despite theatrical and musical textbooks lumping Gilbert and Sullivan with Offenbach, the connections are tenuous at best. The only Gilbert and Sullivan work which resembles *opéra bouffe* is *Thespis*, but it demonstrates a reaction against the French form. When it appeared in 1871, critics were quick to point out its similarities to Offenbach, and one critic went so far as to say, '*Thespis* is quite as good as *Orphée aux Enfers*'.[9] Both works are parodies of mythology and emphasise dance and stage business. Whereas *Orpheus* belittles its gods and goddesses by making them into characters from the Boulevards, *Thespis* achieves the same effect by reducing the deities to Victorian ladies and gentlemen:

> Enter DIANA, an elderly Goddess. She is carefully wrapped up in Cloaks, Shawls, etc. A hood is over her head, a respirator in her mouth, and galoshes on her feet. During the chorus she takes these things off, and discovers herself dressed in the usual costume of the Lunar Diana, the Goddess of the Moon.
> Enter APOLLO. He is an elderly 'buck' with an air of assumed juvenility, and is dressed in dressing gown and smoking cap.

Although Terence Rees has shown similarities between *Thespis* and *La Belle Hélène*, which had been mounted at the same theatre less than eight weeks before, *Thespis* is a Victorian reaction to the excesses of Offenbach.[10] A reason for the theatre's disreputability in the eyes of middle-class Victorians was its importation of French plays; as Jack Point says in *The Yeomen*, a jester could have his wages reduced for telling 'a joke that's too French'. Towards the end of *Thespis* there is a joke made about a Family Edition of Lemprière's classical dictionary, and in many ways *Thespis* can be seen as a kind of Family Edition of Offenbach. Although the stage performance included Nellie Farren in tights in the travesty role of Mercury, the text of the opera is remarkably chaste. While Offenbach's plots turn on sexual intrigue, that of *Thespis* depends on the topsy-turvy idea of gods exchanging places with a troupe of actors. The comedy arises from the consequences of this idea and from satirical one-liners. The spirit of the work is best shown in a song by Mercury who deplores the state of things after the Thespians have taken over:

> In short, you will see from the facts that I'm showing,
> The state of the case is exceedingly sad;
> If Thespis's people go on as they're going.
> Olympus will certainly go to the bad!
> From Jupiter downwards there isn't a dab in it,
> All of 'em quibble and shuffle and shirk;
> A premier in Downing Street, forming a Cabinet,
> Couldn't find people less fit for their work!

Although Sullivan copied many of Offenbach's favourite musical techniques – such as the reprise of previous music – and Gilbert's libretti follow the *opéra comique* formula of spoken dialogue interrupted by music, there is little of the *offenbachiade* in the operas that followed *Thespis*. In Gilbert's eyes at least, Offenbach represented the worst of the English stage at the time. This is made evident in a speech he gave in 1906:

> When Sullivan and I began to collaborate, English comic opera had practically ceased to exist. Such musical entertainments as held the stage were adaptations of the crapulous plots of the operas of Offenbach, Audran, and Lecoq. The plots had generally been Bowdlerized out of intelligibility, and when they had not been subjected to this treatment they were frankly improper; whereas the ladies' dresses suggested that the management had gone on the principle of doing a little and doing it well.

Their collaboration was an attempt to revivify an English light opera tradition. In nineteenth-century

England, there were two operatic traditions. One was that of Italian opera, which found its major home at the King's Theatre and at Covent Garden where a narrow repertoire of operas in Italian was performed according to strict rules of interpretation. So stultifying was the atmosphere at the Italian opera houses that when the successful *English* opera *The Bohemian Girl* was presented in 1858, it had to be translated into Italian and renamed *La Zingara* to satisfy the rules of high operatic art. The second tradition was that of native English opera which had its origin in John Gay's *The Beggar's Opera* (1728), itself written 'to counteract and ridicule the popularity of Italian opera'[11] in the eighteenth century. Gay's innovation consisted of interspersing songs set to pre-existing, familiar tunes throughout the text of a comic play; it became so popular that in the decade following the presentation of *The Beggar's Opera* no less than 120 similar ballad operas were produced. Most of these works had a strongly satirical vein in which contemporary personages and events were ridiculed. Towards the end of the century, the satirical elements evaporated and were replaced by sentiment, melodrama and farce, and the music began to be original, so that the form began more closely to approximate the comic opera.

The native operatic tradition continued into the nineteenth century where it was aided by various schemes to found an English national opera to counterbalance the Italian tradition. As early as 1834, an English Opera House was established, and although it foundered in 1841, it prepared the way for such companies as that run by Louisa Pyne and William Harrison, who sponsored fifteen new English operas from 1856 to 1864. At least eighty original operas in English were produced in London in the period from 1834 to 1865. Although these pieces differed from the ballad opera in that the music was original and the plots melodramatic, they followed the English tradition of arranging a series of musical numbers (songs, ensembles and choruses) within the framework of spoken dialogue. Two of the most popular works from this period were Balfe's *The Bohemian Girl* (1843) and Wallace's *Maritana* (1845) both of which were performed well into the present century. The rest of English opera from this period has quietly disappeared.

Michael Hurd has identified two problems with English opera in this period. The first was the ineptitude of the librettists, generally hacks who derived their plots from popular melodramas and whose lyrics consisted of doggerel 'that would disgrace a Christmas card'. Henry Chorley's libretto for Sullivan's 1863 opera *The Sapphire Necklace*, for example, was described as 'a wretched confusion, utterly lacking in all knowledge of stagecraft and quite unsuitable for any music'. The second hindrance was that music publishers depended on an opera containing songs that could be easily lifted out of context to be published and sold separately for use in the drawing room. The composers of operas in this period did not seem to mind this practice:

> From a composer's point of view an opera was the best way to launch a song. . . . Consequently the songs would be designed for drawing room use out of context, the words would be fairly general in character, and the drama would rarely advance while the music sounded.[12]

Many features of Gilbert and Sullivan's first full-length work after *Thespis*, *The Sorcerer*, are taken from the native English operatic tradition. The setting, the village of Ploverleigh, hearkens back to a whole subtype of ballad opera called village opera which flourished in the eighteenth century. These musical plays, of which the best known example is Arne and Bickerstaffe's *Love in a Village* (1762), take place in the English countryside and depict amorous dallyings amongst the landed gentry against a background of comic scenes drawn from rustic life. In *The Sorcerer*, there are three sets of lovers; the youthful Alexis Pointdextre and Aline Sangazure; their parents, Lady Sangazure and Sir Marmaduke; and Constance, daughter of the village pew-opener and Dr Daly, the vicar. Their romances are played out against a pastoral setting which is richly painted by the chorus of villagers:

MEN: Why, where be oi, and what be oi a doin'
A sleepin' out, just when the dews du rise?
GIRLS: Why, that's the very way your health to ruin,
And don't seem quite respectable likewise!

In this chorus, Gilbert gives the villagers a West Country accent: and the accompanying music together with the subsequent 'Country Dance' is as jollily English as anything in *H.M.S. Pinafore*. No less indicative of the work's English heritage are the large number of 'shop ballads' which are principally assigned to Aline ('Oh happy young heart') and Alexis ('Love feeds on many kinds of food' and 'Thou hast the power thy vaunted love') which would have adorned many a Victorian musical evening.

While in form and musical style the Savoy Operas are descendants of the English romantic tradition, their irreverence is drawn from less respectable ancestry – the burlesques and extravangazas which formed the bulk of mid-Victorian musical entertainment. In 1831, Madame

Vestris took over the Olympic Theatre and engaged James Robinson Planché (1796–1880) as a writer. Prevented from producing straight plays by the monopoly that Covent Garden and Drury Lane held on the presentation of legitimate (i.e. purely spoken) drama, Vestris and Planché determined 'to raise the "illegitimate" forms to a plane of excellence unsurpassed in the memories of her older patrons'. The first pieces that Planché prepared for Madame Vestris were classical burlesques such as *Olympic Revels*, or *Prometheus and Pandora* (1831) and *The Paphian Bower*, or *Venus and Adonis* (1832) in which, as Augustin Filon puts it, 'the whole point of the piece consists in putting modern sentiments and expressions into the mouths of characters taken from antiquity'.[13] These entertainments were written in rhyming couplets, interspersed with songs sung to popular tunes of the day, and produced with a discipline then rare on the English stage. An example of Planché's mature work in this form is *The Golden Fleece* which was produced at the Haymarket in 1845. At times, this work reads like a translation of Euripides' *Medea*, but its facetious tone is exemplified by a note in the Dramatis Personae:

> N.B. The public is respectfully informed, that in order to produce this Grand Classical work in a style which may defy comparison in any other establishment, the lessee has, regardless of expense, engaged
> MR. CHARLES MATHEWS
> to represent the whole body of the chorus, rendering at least fifty-nine male voices entirely unnecessary.

Towards the end of the play, when Medea disappears offstage supposedly to kill her children, screams are heard from within the palace, but it turns out that this is because instead of killing them she has decided to send them to a grammar school.

By the 1860s, such writers as F. C. Burnand, H. J. Byron and Francis Talfourd broadened the scope of burlesque so that its targets included not only classical myths but also history, literary classics and contemporary operatic and theatrical successes. Beginning with *Dulcamara* (a burlesque of Donizetti's *L'Elisir d'Amore*) in 1866, Gilbert contributed a number of pieces to the burlesque form. An example of Gilbert's burlesque and of mid-Victorian musical entertainment in general, is his *Robert the Devil; Or The Nun, The Dun, and the Son of a Gun*. In 1868, John Hollingshead began management of the Gaiety Theatre, and for the opening night, 26 December 1868, commissioned Gilbert to write a burlesque of Meyerbeer's opera *Robert le Diable*. The opening night programme shows the endurance of Victorian audiences, for not only did it include Gilbert's piece (which ran to five acts) but also an operetta (translated from the French) called *The Two Harlequins* and a three act comedy-drama adapted from the French called *On the Cards*.[14] Gilbert's object of satire was Meyerbeer's popular opera, first produced in Paris in 1831. During the course of the original opera, Robert is persuaded by Bertram (the villain) that the only way to win the heart of his beloved, Princess Isabella, is to commit the sacrilege of stealing a branch of a magic bough from a tomb in a deserted cloister. In the climactic scene, a chorus of ghostly nuns incite Robert to steal the branch. Subsequently, Robert uses it to overpower Isabella's keepers, but when she persuades him to break the branch, he is captured.

In Gilbert's *Robert the Devil*, songs set to tunes by

Curtain-Raiser: the Theatrical Background

Bellini, Auber, Offenbach, Hervé and Javelot replaced the original score. The Cloister Scene is set in the Chamber of Horrors at Madame Tussaud's, where the wax figures come to life and perform a ballet. During the dance Robert snatches the magic branch – which turns out to be a policeman's truncheon. This prefigures the portrait gallery scene in *Ruddigore* twenty years later. This is how the Chorus of Wax-Works foreshadows the Ghosts of *Ruddigore*:

> We're only wax-work,
> With hair of flax-work,
> And dressed in sack's work,
> Artistic quack's work;
> With clumsy rack's work,
> Our arms and backs work. – Oh! (*wildly*)
> (*Reassuringly to audience*)
> Now pray don't run,
> That's but our fun!
> At midnight hour,
> When thunder lower,
> And lightnings glower,
> And torrents shower,
> It's in our power
> To leave our bower. – Oh.
> You needn't be
> Alarmed at me,
> Because you see,
> I'm only wax-work, etc.

The humour of *Robert the Devil* lies in its comic juxtaposition of allusions to Meyerbeer's opera and elements (such as the Chamber of Horrors) which are drawn from the everyday world of the audience. Such juxtaposition is one of the informing principles of burlesque; it is also one of the chief elements in the Savoy Operas. When Ko-Ko tells the Mikado that Nanki-Poo's name 'might have been on his pocket handkerchief, but Japanese don't use pocket handkerchiefs' the humour is created by this unexpected reference to the commonplace in the midst of an exotic setting. At the opening of *Ruddigore*, the chorus of bridesmaids sings sweetly about the virtues of Rose Maybud, and just as we are lulled into accepting their cloying innocence, we find out that they are 'an endowed corps of professional bridesmaids who are bound to be on duty every day from ten to four'. Sullivan plays the same type of prank in his scores: the entrance of the Judge in *Trial by Jury* is accompanied by a mock-Handelian chorus. This deflation of the serious and the sentimental is summed up by Bunthorne in *Patience*:

Do you know what it is to yearn for the Indefinable, and yet to be brought, face to face, daily, with the Multiplication Table? Do you know what it is to seek oceans and find puddles? – to long for whirlwinds and yet have to do the best you can with the bellows?

Another Victorian theatrical form which influenced the Savoy Operas was the fairy extravaganza. Rather than debunk a legend or myth, the extravaganza sought to retell a fairy-tale or whimsical story in as delightful a manner as possible. Of mid-Victorian fairy extravaganza, William Brough's *Prince Amabel or The Fairy Roses* (1862) is typical. Prince Amabel is in love with a girl whom he sees only in his dreams. A Fairy gives him magic roses that confer on him the power of invisibility so that he may find his love. The roses help Amabel reach the kingdom of the tyrant Turko, whose daughter turns out to be the girl of his dreams. After several adventures, Amabel wins her hand, and the piece concludes with a spectacular 'Vision of the Flowery Future'. *Prince Amabel*, like most other burlesques and extravaganzas, is written in rhyming couplets and the dialogue is riddled with puns:

FAIRY: I am a fairy.
PRINCE: So I should have guessed.
　　　 By the amount of gauze in which you're
　　　　 dressed.
FAIRY: Is it effective?
PRINCE: Yes, by Nature's laws,
　　　 There's no effect without sufficient gauze.

The work is punctuated with songs set to popular airs and many of the lyrics are worthy of Gilbert, such as Turko's song:

I'll sing a good old song of the monarch truly great,
The fine old-fashioned tyrant of the school legitimate,
Who scorns the namby-pamby rule of kings effeminate,
And much above his subjects' love, prefers his people's
　　 hate.

Like other extravaganzas, to a twentieth-century reader *Prince Amabel* is reminiscent of the modern British pantomime. The original form of the pantomime was a short Opening based on a fairy-tale followed by a Transformation Scene in which the characters were changed into the figures of Harlequin, Columbine, Clown and Pantaloon. These figures then romped through a lengthy Harlequinade. In *Harlequin in his Element*, David

Mayer attributes the decline of this traditional form after 1836 to the rise in popularity of the fairy extravaganza. The pantomime Opening was lengthened until it, not the Harlequinade, was the chief element – as it is today. This is well illustrated by the titles of the Christmas pantomimes written by Henry Saville for the Theatre Royal at Nottingham: the fare at Christmas 1863 was *Harlequin Prince Thalaba, or Queen Khawla, the Enchantress, and the Fairy Bells of Paradise*.

Gilbert was very fond of the pantomime, and magic is one of the recurring motifs in the Savoy Operas. In many operas, the supernatural is overtly presented, as in the Incantation Scene of *The Sorcerer* and the ghost sequence in *Ruddigore*.With its fairy chorus tripping hither and thither and its magical transformation of mortals into fairies, *Iolanthe* is strongly reminiscent of pantomime. Even in operas with no obvious supernatural element, characters have magical associations: Colonel Fairfax in *The Yeomen* dabbles in alchemy and Little Buttercup in *Pinafore* has gypsy blood in her veins. A feeling of magic is never far beneath the surface in any of the operas. Events are often dictated by forces outside the characters' control and people are given strange or unusual powers. Gilbert's notes on *The Pirates of Penzance*, for example, suggest that the policeman's repetition of 'Tarantara' is meant to be a kind of magical chant: 'The police always sing "Tarantara" when they desire to work their courage to sticking point. They are naturally timid, but through the agency of this talisman they are able to acquit themselves when concealed.'

The Savoy Operas are a hybridisation of pre-existing elements from the British theatre. In his libretti, Gilbert combined the magic and whimsy of the extravaganza with the irreverence of the burlesque and the nonsense spirit of his German Reed entertainments. Sullivan's scores wedded the ballad opera tradition to the vitality of Offenbach. This mixture of ingredients makes classification of the operas difficult, a problem recognised by *Punch* in November 1884:

It is difficult to classify these Gilbert–Sullivan operas. They are not, strictly speaking, Comic Operas, they are not operettas, they are not exactly German Reed Entertainments, nor Extravaganzas, nor Burlesques. What are they?

Punch's answer is still valid today:

They are perfectly original, and Messrs. Gilbert and Sullivan have founded a school of their own. Once upon a time Messrs. Bunn and Balfe were the chief Professors of a style of entertainment called 'Ballad Operas'. Now, as the plots of *The Sorcerer*, *Pinafore*, *Patience* and *Pirates*, remind me of the grotesque humour of the *Bab Ballads*, I should suggest that the Gilbert–Sullivan series should be known as The Bab Ballad Operas.

3
The Masterpiece: 'The Mikado'

The Savoy Operas can be divided into two broad groups whose differences are apparent in listing the settings for the operas (see table, pp. x–xi). Excluding *Thespis*, the first six operas – from *Trial by Jury* to *Iolanthe* – are set in Victorian England. Their action is contemporary with the time of their composition, and they are full of elements drawn directly from the world of the London theatre audience of the 1880s: a police sergeant, a courtroom, the Palace Yard at Westminster, a regiment of Dragoons, a country vicar, a ship's company of sailors, a Major-General in the British Army, and so on. Beginning with *Princess Ida*, the operas are set in times and places increasingly remote from Britain in the 1880s: Japan, Tudor England, eighteenth-century Italy, a South Pacific kingdom and a German principality. This shift in setting coincides with a decrease in social satire. The first six operas satirise various aspects of Victorian life, but in the later operas satire is diluted by increasing emphasis on music, comic characterisation and spectacle.

The Mikado (1881) was written mid-way through the twenty-year collaboration of Gilbert and Sullivan, and it has features drawn from both the early and late operas. Ostensibly, it is set in Japan. The Oriental locale may have been inspired by Offenbach and Halevy's *Ba-Ta-Clan* of 1855, a comic musical piece set in China in which the leading characters (one of whom is called Ko-ko-ri-ko) turn out to be marooned Frenchmen. This work had been played at the Gallery of Illustration as *Ching-Chow-Hi*. A craze for things Japanese swept fashionable England in the 1880s. This reached its apogee in 1885 with a Japanese Exhibition in Knightsbridge (made reference to in the second act where Ko-Ko reports Nanki-Poo's address as 'Knightsbridge'); here the top-hatted and crinolined onlookers could marvel at the curious dress and customs of the Japanese, so completely different from their own. Victorian bemusement with foreign customs is shown in the opening chorus of *The Mikado*, where the Japanese gentlemen sing, 'our attitude's queer and quaint – You're wrong if you think it ain't'. But you only have to listen to the overture to realise that the biggest joke in the opera is the setting. After a few bars of pseudo-Oriental music, the overture switches to the completely English idiom of 'The sun whose rays'. Although the characters wear Japanese dress and make-up, their manners, speech and attitudes are utterly Victorian. When Yum-Yum tells Nanki-Poo that 'I'm right at the top of the school, and I've got three prizes', she sounds like any English schoolgirl; and the instrument played by Nanki-Poo in the Titipu Town Band – the trombone – is decidedly un-Oriental.

This hybridisation of Oriental setting with Victorian

characters makes *The Mikado* a transitional work that marks the boundary between the satiric mode of the early operas and the romantic mode of the later ones. Its blend of topicality and fantasy combine the best features of the early and late Gilbert and Sullivan, and therefore it provides a useful starting-place for discussion of the operas.

Like all of the operas except *The Yeomen*, the piece opens with a chorus introducing the setting and situation. At curtain rise, the audience discovers a group of Japanese nobles 'standing and sitting in attitudes suggested by native drawings'. The chorus is made up of males only; this is reflected in the robustness of the music. A minority of the thirteen Gilbert and Sullivan operas begin with a mixed (both male and female) chorus. In the others, the opera opens with a chorus of one sex and the entrance of the chorus of the opposite sex is delayed until halfway through the first act. The male and female choruses usually represent antithetical elements whose clash provides a background for the conflicts of the main characters. As the opera proceeds, these antithetical elements are reconciled and usually the male and female choruses are joined in matrimony at the conclusion. Such a pattern is seen with the pirates and Major-General Stanley's daughters in *The Pirates*, the rapturous maidens and dragoons in *Patience*, and the fairies and Peers in *Iolanthe*. The reconciliation of choruses is, however, not seen in *H.M.S. Pinafore*, where presumably the forces of class distinction are too great to forge a bond between the sailors and Sir Joseph's sisters, cousins and aunts. In *The Mikado*, there is no overt dramatic conflict between the male and female choruses, but they still represent divergent forces. The Japanese nobles, with their strict adherence to 'Court etiquette', contrast to the schoolgirls, 'filled to the brim with girlish glee'. The implication is of a conflict between generations.

Gilbert's opening choruses often foreshadow events and themes in the opera. Two important images are presented in the opening chorus of *The Mikado*. The first is that of artificiality:

> On many a vase and jar –
> On many a screen and fan,
> We figure in lively paint:
> Our attitude's queer and quaint

This verbal image is reinforced by the visual one of the chorus 'standing and sitting in attitudes suggested by native drawings'. In several previous works, Gilbert used the device of a work of art coming to life: in *Robert the Devil*, a waxworks gallery; in *Ages Ago*, a portrait gallery; and in *Pygmalion and Galatea*, a statue. A similar idea is more subtly suggested in the opening moments of *The Mikado*. Modern productions of *The Mikado* often begin with the nobles frozen in various attitudes and then coming to life one by one. The implicit statement is that the characters in the opera are not real but part of a fantasy played out by figures on a Japanese vase who magically come alive. The audience slips into the world of the Japanese vase as easily as Alice slips through the mirror, and the world encountered, every bit as fantastic as the Looking-Glass world, has a kind of perverse dream-like symmetry. At the beginning of Act II, the female chorus reiterates the same idea:

> Paint the pretty face –
> Dye the coral lip –
> Emphasise the grace

Of her Ladyship!
Art and nature, thus allied,
Go to make a pretty bride.

The second important image in the opening chorus is
that of a puppet:

If you think we are worked by strings,
Like a Japanese marionette,
You don't understand these things:
It is simply Court etiquette.

The image of people as marionettes occurs in another
opera, *Patience*, when the dragoons attempt to adopt
the mannerisms of aestheticism:

To cultivate the trim
Rigidity of limb,
You ought to get a Marionette, and form your style on
him.

Such images are used to satirise the characters' conformity
to particular styles of behaviour: etiquette in the case of
the nobles and aestheticism in the case of the dragoons.
Unthinking rigid adherence to rules of social behaviour is
a theme which surfaces to a greater or lesser extent in all
of the operas. In *The Pirates*, it is seen in Frederic's blind
devotion to duty; in *Ruddigore*, in Rose Maybud's
constant reference to her book of etiquette. This idea
serves the dual purpose of a comic and satirical device:
the characters' conformity forces them into absurd
situations which are funny for their own sake and also
provide a satirical reflection of human society – in
particular, Victorian society with its elaborate codes of

deportment and behaviour. *The Mikado* presents a whole society in which everyone's behaviour is governed by laws emanating from the Mikado, and much of the comedy of the opera derives from the characters' deviousness in circumventing the law.

The vase painting and marionette images of the opening chorus predict the artificiality of the opera's structure. Events in *The Mikado* occur with a mechanical precision that is both unreal and entertaining for its own sake. The construction of the piece is based on the principles of the well-made play. In the early nineteenth century, the French dramatist Eugene Scribe (1791–1861) transformed playwriting into a craft in which plays were assembled from a stockpile of situations, plots and characters. One critic has enumerated fifty-five stock situations each of which may occur up to twenty-five times in the plays of Scribe.[1] An example of such a stock situation is a girl loving a man above her social station, which occurs in no less than seventeen of Scribe's comic operas. The pieces that resulted from this method were called *pièces bien fait*, or well-made plays, because the emphasis lay not so much on character or theme as on the arrangement and timing of events. Characteristically, such a play begins at a late point in the story, and opens with an exposition outlining the events which have preceded the play's action. The rest of the play consists of a carefully arranged string of events which alter the fortunes of the play's hero in a see-saw pattern. Usually, there is a major misunderstanding between characters which is obvious to the audience but is withheld from the characters until the end. Other devices include coincidental meetings, the arrival of unexpected and surprising news, and the revelation of a long-suppressed secret. Although these devices of discovery and reversal had been used in western drama since the time of Aristotle, in the hand of Scribe they were honed to perfection.

Scribe's influence can be found everywhere in nineteenth-century drama. In serious drama, it is in the exciting alternation of success and misfortune that befall the heroes of melodrama; in comedy, its influence is in farce. The essence of nineteenth-century farce is the cleverness of arrangement of the events of the plot: misunderstandings, disguises, deceits, revelations, secrets, discoveries, coincidences and errors are crammed into a time framework which pressurises events to an absurd and bewildering level. In the mid-Victorian theatre, the favoured position of farce in an evening's entertainment was the 'curtain-raiser' – a short, snappy piece in one act designed to warm the audience to the main fare of the evening. The most prolific and successful writer of curtain raisers at mid-century was John Maddison Morton (1811–91) whose work unquestionably stimulated Gilbert's nonsense streak. The tone of Morton's pieces is suggested by their titles: *Slasher and Crasher*, *Grimshaw, Bagshaw and Bradshaw* and *Box and Cox* are but three examples. The latter play, a skilful interweaving of two French farces, revolves around a set of absurd coincidences. Mrs Bouncer rents a room to two lodgers, Mr Cox who works all day, and Mr Box who works at night, and so she gets double rent for her room. During the course of the play, the inevitable happens: Mr Cox encounters Mr Box, and from then on ridiculous coincidences occur in rapid succession. Both men turn out to have been wooed by the same woman, Penelope Ann, and both have tried to escape her affections. The best coincidence is saved for last:

BOX: You'll excuse the apparent insanity of the remark,

but the more I gaze on your features, the more I'm
convinced that you're my long-lost brother.

COX: The very observation I was going to make to you!

BOX: Ah, tell me – in mercy tell me – have you such a
thing as a strawberry mark on your left arm?

COX: No!

BOX: Then it is he![2]

During his early dramatic career, Gilbert wrote a
number of one-act farces similar to Morton's, but his real
apprenticeship in the form came in his adaptation-
translations of lengthier French farces in the early 1870s.
Gilbert himself had much to do with the introduction of
the three-act French farce to the English stage: as Michael
Booth notes: '*The Wedding March* (1873), Gilbert's
version of *Un Chapeau de Paille d'Italie* (1851), by
Eugène Labiche and Marc-Michel, really began the vogue
of adaptation from . . . French farce.'[3] In 1873, he
rendered translations of *Le Réveillon* by Offenbach's
librettists Meilhac and Halevy, and Labiche and Marc-
Michel's *La Dame aux Jambes d'Azur*.

The meticulous construction of the Savoy Operas
suggests that he was stimulated by the clockwork-like
precision of these French farces. *The Mikado* demonstrates
many techniques of the well-made play. To begin with,
much of the story has taken place before the opera
begins; a full one-third of the first act is taken up with
recapitulation of prior events. Gilbert's exposition is
deliberate and methodical. Following the introduction of
the male chorus and Nanki-Poo, we learn from the
dialogue that the story extends back a year in time, when
Nanki-Poo fell in love with Yum-Yum. Unfortunately,
Yum-Yum was engaged to her guardian, Ko-Ko, and so
Nanki-Poo did not press his suit. Hearing that Ko-Ko has

been condemned to death for flirting, he has now returned to Titipu in hopes of wooing Yum-Yum. The first important new piece of information is that Ko-Ko has been reprieved and is still a threat to Nanki-Poo. This news is provided by Pish-Tush in his song, 'Our great Mikado'. Next, with the arrival of Pooh-Bah, we learn that (by amazing coincidence!) today is the day that Yum-Yum and Ko-Ko, who has been raised to the post of Lord High Executioner, are to be married. This is also presented in a song: 'Young man, despair'. Each key piece of information is thus emphasised by the arrival of a new character and by a song. Just in case anyone has missed anything, Nanki-Poo summarises the exposition to this point:

> And have I journeyed for a month, or nearly,
> To learn that Yum-Yum, whom I love so dearly,
> This day to Ko-Ko is to be united!

The subsequent action depends on the careful timing of revelations of key bits of information and appearances by characters at opportune moments. We learn that Nanki-Poo is in reality the son of the Mikado and has fled his father's court to escape the attention of Katisha, an elderly lady 'who has claimed him in marriage'. The important event in the middle part of Act I is the unexpected arrival of a letter from the Mikado: he demands that an execution be performed in Titipu. When Nanki-Poo declares his intention to kill himself for love of Yum-Yum, Ko-Ko persuades him to offer himself as a candidate for public execution. In return, Nanki-Poo can marry Yum-Yum until his death. This agreement solves a dilemma for both men – Nanki-Poo gets Yum-Yum and Ko-Ko gets his execution – and the first act ends in a celebration which is marred only by the melodramatic appearance of Katisha, who is seeking Nanki-Poo.

The second act begins with a revelation that completely overturns the state of affairs at the end of Act I. When it is discovered that by the Mikado's law she must be buried with Nanki-Poo when he dies, Yum-Yum breaks off her engagement to Nanki-Poo, who is plunged again into suicidal despair. The announcement by Pooh-Bah that the Mikado's arrival is imminently expected pressurises the action to farcical rapidity. Ko-Ko quickly arranges a subterfuge that will satisfy all parties. He has Nanki-Poo killed 'by affidavit' – that is, he simply prepares a document testifying that Nanki-Poo has been executed. In return for this, Ko-Ko waives his rights to Yum-Yum and she is allowed to marry Nanki-Poo. Once again order seems to have been restored, but then the Mikado arrives and discovers that Ko-Ko has executed his son. He condemns Ko-Ko and his accomplice to death. The only way out is for Nanki-Poo to come forward and declare that he is not dead, but he refuses to do so for fear of Katisha. The final solution is for Ko-Ko to woo and wed Katisha, which he does, and with Katisha out of the way Nanki-Poo is able to come forward and show his father that he has not been slain.

As this summary shows, the plot of *The Mikado* is composed from standard farcical devices of deception, disguise, misunderstanding and coincidence. Beneath this farcical mask the opera displays many classical features of comedy. As Northrop Frye points out in *The Anatomy of Criticism*, since Roman times western comedy has been remarkably consistent in content and approach.[4] In the comedies of Plautus, Shakespeare, Molière or Sheridan, the same basic story is told: a young man loves a young woman, and his efforts to obtain her are opposed and obstructed by other characters. The action of the play centres upon the efforts of these characters (often parents, often rivals) to block the fulfilment of the hero's wishes. At the end of the comedy, the obstacles are removed, the young man gets the young woman, and festivity and happiness ensue. 'Boy gets girl' and 'They both lived happily ever after' are trite phrases, but they express neatly the two main ingredients of stage comedy.

This universal comic blueprint is easy to recognise in *The Mikado*. Nanki-Poo and Yum-Yum are lovers, and their union is obstructed by two rivals, Ko-Ko who loves Yum-Yum and Katisha who loves Nanki-Poo. The change in relationship of this quartet of characters is the main dramatic action of the opera. At the beginning, the relationship may be depicted schematically:

Ko-Ko   Katisha
  ↓ loves   ↓ loves
Yum-Yum ←————— loves —————→ Nanki-Poo

From the outset, it is clear that this is a wrong ordering. For one thing, neither the love of Ko-Ko for Yum-Yum nor that of Katisha for Nanki-Poo is reciprocated: Yum-Yum states quite emphatically that she does not love Ko-Ko, and Nanki-Poo says that all he feels for Katisha is his 'customary affability'. There is also the age of the characters. Katisha is described as 'an elderly lady' and Ko-Ko is old enough to be Yum-Yum's guardian. Despite the obvious unnaturalness of these partnerships, the opera opens in the hours before Yum-Yum and Ko-Ko's wedding.

The solution found during the course of the opera involves the removal of Ko-Ko and Katisha as rivals to the younger lovers. This is accomplished through Ko-Ko relinquishing Yum-Yum in return for Nanki-Poo's agreement to allow himself to die by affidavit, and by Katisha being tricked into thinking that Nanki-Poo has been killed, thus leaving herself free to be wooed and won by Ko-Ko. There is a neat irony to the fact that the two blocking characters are removed as obstacles to the young lovers by their own union, which leaves the relationship at the end of the opera as:

Ko-Ko $\longleftrightarrow$ Katisha
Yum-Yum $\longleftrightarrow$ Nanki-Poo

This new pairing seems the right ordering. Not only is Nanki-Poo and Yum-Yum's love fulfilled, but the reluctant marraige between Ko-Ko and Katisha is a comic punishment for both of them. The obstacles are overcome, the youthful lovers triumph, and the opera ends with images of rebirth:

YUM-YUM AND NANKI-POO: The threatened cloud has
passed away,
And brightly shines the
dawning day;
What though the night may
come too soon,
We've years and years of
afternoon!

ALL: Then let the throng
Our joy advance,
With laughing song
And merry dance,
With joyous shouts and
ringing cheer,
Inaugurate our new career!

Similar images of renewal are found in the other operas, which follow the same comic pattern as *The Mikado*. The first act introduces a group of characters who are thrust into a dilemma which seems insoluble. Most often, this dilemma arises from the separation of two lovers by external forces. At the end of the first act, a temporary solution to the dilemma is found and the act curtain falls amid celebration. In the second act, the ending of the first act is shown to be a false happy ending, for new complications arise to destroy the validity of the temporary solution. During the course of the second act, a new solution is found which results in a true happy ending involving the marriage of the lovers. In many of the operas, the false happy ending is interrupted by a figure who foreshadows the unhappiness of the second act. The universality of this pattern can be seen by comparing *The Mikado* with *H.M.S. Pinafore*, where the central dilemma is the love of the sailor Ralph for his Captain's daughter. At the end of the first act the lovers decide to elope, but their happiness is undercut by the appearance of Dick Deadeye, who is later to foil their plans. In the second act, the lovers suffer a setback when Captain Corcoran and Sir Joseph Porter discover the elopement, but at the end of the opera these obstacles are removed and the couple are married. The closing number is similar to *The Mikado*:

> Oh joy, oh rapture unforeseen,
> The clouded sky is now serene,
> The god of day – the orb of love,
> Has hung his ensign high above,
> The sky is all ablaze.

A dissection of the structure of *The Mikado* shows that each part reflects the whole: the opera is assembled from small units each of which has its own exposition, denouement and conclusion. Each of these units of dramatic action consists of a stretch of dialogue plus one or two musical numbers. During the dialogue, the characters introduce a new problem which they solve through application of deception, disguise or scheme. The scene ends with a musical number reiterating and commenting on the events and ideas of the scene. Following the musical number, the stage is cleared in readiness for new characters and new problems. For example, in the scene following the Mikado's exit in Act II, the characters are faced with the problem of how Nanki-Poo can reveal his identity to his father without invoking Katisha's wrath. After discussion, they decide that the best way out is for Ko-Ko to wed Katisha. This decided, they launch into a song – 'The flowers that bloom in the spring' – in which they express their differing attitudes to the decision: Nanki-Poo looks forward to a 'summer of roses and wine' while Ko-Ko despairs at the prospect of marrying a 'most unattractive old thing'. The characters dance off (dances provide the punctuation marks between dramatic units) and Katisha enters. Despairing at the loss of Nanki-Poo, she sings a lament. Ko-Ko then enters. His job is to find some way of winning her over, which he does by singing 'Tit-willow'. Katisha agrees to marry him, and the scene ends with a happy duet and – as usual – a dance. The pace of the opera in performance depends very much on the director's and performers' awareness of these units.

One of the reasons why *The Mikado* is Gilbert and Sullivan's masterpiece is that the cohesion between music and drama is complete. Songs are not simply 'tacked on' the end of scenes but are an integral part of the expression of the dramatic situation. The best example is the trio sung by Ko-Ko, Pish-Tush and Pooh-Bah in Act I. In the preceding scene, the three have learned that the Mikado wants an execution to be carried out in Titipu. The song begins with a solo by each man in which he expresses his reasons why he should not be the victim. Then the three men sing together, each singing different words to a different melody, so that the overall effect on the ear is discordance and confusion – a vivid musical reinforcement of the disagreements between the characters.

In many operas the obstacles to the lovers' union are not just individual characters but abstract principles or ideas. In *The Pirates*, for example, Mabel and Frederic are separated not so much by any objection from Major-General Stanley as by Frederic's adherence to duty. Ralph and Josephine in *Pinafore* are forbidden to marry because they are of different social classes; they are united only when Ralph turns out to be of higher class than he appears. *Patience* is more complicated as there is a chain of unrequited love: the dragoons love the maidens who love Bunthorne who loves Patience who loves (for part of the time, anyway) Grosvenor. The obstacles to the dragoons' love for the maidens is aestheticism; as Lady Saphir says to the Colonel:

> You are not Empyrean. You are not Della Cruscan. You are not even Early English. Oh, be Early English ere it is too late.

Patience refuses to return Bunthorne's love because of her idealistic expectations that true love must be unselfish; in loving him she would be robbing the world of his perfection. In *Princess Ida*, the childhood romance between Ida and Hilarion is prevented from reaching fulfilment by Ida's feminist repudiation of men. Duty, class, aestheticism, idealism, feminism: these are some of the social forces that block love in the Savoy Operas.

In *The Mikado*, the union of the lovers is blocked not just by Ko-Ko and Katisha but also by the laws of the Mikado himself. Although he does not physically appear until the second act, the Mikado is the most powerful figure in the opera. His presence is felt right from the start of Act I, when Pish-Tush describes the law against flirting. From then on, his offstage decrees are the main stimulus to the characters' behaviour. Yum-Yum and Nanki-Poo are prevented from expressing their affection for one another because of the 'excessively severe' laws against flirting; their marriage is to be cut short by the execution of Nanki-Poo in accordance with the Mikado's decree; and Yum-Yum breaks off the engagement when she learns that by the Mikado's law she must die with Nanki-Poo.

The opera presents a world where human behaviour is carefully regulated and controlled. Two of the most familiar songs, Ko-Ko's 'As some day it may happen' and the Mikado's 'A more humane Mikado', are catalogues of behaviours punishable under the law. In these songs, the Japanese facade of the opera splits open, for the crimes and punishments listed are, for the most part, distinctively Victorian. Ko-Ko's little list of 'society offenders who might well be underground' includes 'the lady from the provinces, who dresses like a guy,/And who "doesn't think she dances, but would rather like to try" '. The Mikado's list of punishments includes some that by their topicality have lost their meaning in the twentieth century. While we still understand the justice of sending the amateur tenor to practise at Madame Tussaud's waxwork, the reason for making the railway carriage graffiti artist ride on 'Parliamentary trains' is much less clear.[5] Such topicality anchors the opera firmly in Victorian England, and suggests that it is Gilbert and Sullivan's own society, with its insistence on rules of etiquette and deportment, that is being slyly presented.

The Mikado himself is a Victorian character: he is not so much a political ruler as a dispenser of public morality. He tells us at his entrance that 'my morals have been declared/Particularly correct', and his puritanical zeal is revealed in the decree against flirting, which is part of 'a plan whereby/Young men might best be steadied'. He expects obedience from every man, but governs 'in a fatherly kind of way'. These images suggest a Victorian papa, watching gently but firmly over the conduct of his family; taken one step further, they suggest that the Mikado is an oblique caricature of Queen Victoria, whose behaviour served as a moral beacon for an empire.

The Mikado is the most powerful figure in the opera not only because he is the ruler of the country and father of the hero but because he is associated with death. *The Mikado* is a comic opera, but references to death occur in every scene. Most of the chief characters are under threat of execution at one time or another – not very pleasant executions either: decapitation, burying alive and boiling in oil are but three choices. Nanki-Poo twice threatens to commit suicide on stage; and Ko-Ko's song 'Tit-willow' tells of the suicide of a love-sick bird. Images of death occur repeatedly in the songs: among the most potent is the chorus from the Act I trio:

> To sit in solemn silence in a dull, dark dock,
> In a pestilential prison, with a life-long lock,
> Awaiting the sensation of a short, sharp shock,
> From a cheap and chippy chopper on a big black
>   block!

Pooh-Bah's description of a decapitated head is the stuff of nightmares:

> Now though you'd have said that head was dead
> (For its owner dead was he),
> It stood on its neck, with a smile well-bred,
> And bowed three times to me!

The awareness of death's 'short, sharp shock' creates a mood of nervous terror that enhances the comedy. It also results in an undercurrent of sadness and pessimism. The philosophical outlook of the opera is summed up by the Mikado when he says, 'I'm really very sorry for you all, but it's an unjust world, and virtue is triumphant only in theatrical performances.' The opera does present a ruthless, unjust world dominated by laws and decrees that are as arbitrary as they are extreme. In one scene, Ko-Ko celebrates his engagement to Yum-Yum; in the next, his mood changes to anxiety when a letter from the Mikado arrives demanding an execution. The Mikado's power is devastating: unless the execution is performed, Ko-Ko will be stripped of his title and Titipu will be reduced in rank from a town to a village. As Pish-Tush notes, this will cause 'irretrievable ruin' for everyone. The Glee in the second act expresses the characters' awareness of the injustices of life:

> See how the Fates their gifts allot,
> For A is happy – B is not.
> Yet B is worthy, I dare say,
> Of more prosperity than A!

In this setting of comedy within the framework of harsh law Gilbert is following a tradition of comedy. *A Midsummer Night's Dream*, for example, opens with

Egeus' complaint that his daughter Hermia refuses to wed Demetrius. His ruthlessness is horrifying:

> I beg the ancient privilege of Athens;
> As she is mine, I may dispose of her,
> Which shall be either to this gentleman
> Or to her death, according to our law
> Immediately provided in that case.

A few lines later, Theseus, the Duke of Athens, says that Hermia's penalty will be: 'Either to die the death, or to abjure/For ever the society of men.'

The Mikado presents a society no less strict than that of Shakespeare's Athens. Exactly the same situation has occurred; the Mikado has ordered his son to marry Katisha or be executed, and just as the lovers in *A Midsummer Night's Dream* flee Athens, so Nanki-Poo flees his father's court. The difference is that while at the end of Shakespeare's play Theseus softens his tone, at the end of *The Mikado* there is no evidence that the Mikado has become a more clement ruler. Unlike Ko-Ko and Katisha, the Mikado undergoes no real or symbolic punishment for his role in keeping the lovers apart. One has the impression that it will be business as usual for the Lord High Executioner of Titipu on the next day.

One response of Gilbert's characters to the unjust world around them is resignation and stoicism expressed in the Madrigal at the opening of the second act:

> Brightly dawns our wedding day;
> Joyous hour, we give thee greeting!
> Whither, whither are thou fleeing?
> Fickle moment, prithee stay!
> What though mortal joys be hollow?
> Pleasures come, if sorrows follow:

> Though the tocsin sound, ere long,
> Ding dong! Ding dong!
> Yet until the shadows fall
> Over one and over all,
> Sing a merry madrigal –
> A madrigal!

This stoicism makes *The Mikado* a characteristically late-Victorian work. The attitude of the Madrigal is found in other literature of the period,[6] and its root is the spiritual crisis of the mid-nineteenth century. At mid-century, traditional religious thought concerning man's origin and purpose was challenged by advancements in scientific thinking. In particular, Darwin's theory of evolution overturned the idea of man as a favoured being created by God and replaced it with the view that he is nothing but the highest form of animal life. He has got to the top not by divine providence but by the ruthless mechanism of natural selection. Like other animals, he is at the mercy of natural laws which lack logic or compassion. In the face of this intellectual onslaught, many Victorians clung even more strongly to religious faith; but others such as Matthew Arnold could only watch with sadness as the sea of faith retreated. At the end of 'Dover Beach' (1851) he makes the classic statement about the modern world:

> . . . the world, which seems
> To lie before us like a land of dreams,
> So various, so beautiful, so new,
> Hath really neither joy, nor love, nor light,
> Nor certitude, nor peace, nor help for pain;
> And we are here as on a darkling plain
> Swept with confused alarms of struggle and flight,
> Where ignorant armies clash by night.

Pooh-Bah's description of his ancestry – 'a protoplasmal primordial atomic globule' – is a reminder that *The Mikado* was written in the post-Darwin era. The dark undertones of death and despair are a reflection of late-nineteenth-century pessimism: even in the concluding chorus of the opera the general mood of happiness is qualified by the thought that 'night may come too soon'.

What makes the opera a comedy and not a tragedy is the relentless ingenuity of the characters in overcoming the injustices of the world. Although the Mikado is not defeated at the end of the opera, the characters do get what they want: Nanki-Poo gets Yum-Yum, and Ko-Ko and Pooh-Bah preserve their lives. Gilbert's characters are cerebral beings who use their intellects to achieve their goals without outwardly disturbing the social order. Such cleverness is shown by Pish-Tush when he describes how the citizens of Titipu have circumvented the laws against flirting:

> And so we straight let out on bail
> A convict from the county jail,
> Whose head was next
> On some pretext
> Condemned to be mown off,
> And made him headsman, for we said,
> 'Who's next to be decapited
> Cannot cut off another's head
> Until he's cut his own off.'

Later in the opera, Nanki-Poo and Yum-Yum manage to flirt without actually disobeying the law by demonstrating to each other how they would behave if the law did not exist. The final speech of the opera, in which Ko-Ko explains Nanki-Poo's 'death' to the Mikado, is a consummate example of this sophistry:

> It's like this: When your Majesty says, 'Let a thing be done,' it's as good as done – practically, it is done – because your Majesty's will is law. Your Majesty says, 'Kill a gentleman', and a gentleman is told off to be killed. Consequently, that gentleman is as good as dead – practically, he is dead – and if he is dead, why not say so?

The same mechanism operates in all these examples: the characters find some means of transgressing the law while simultaneously maintaining outward conformity. This discrepancy between outer conduct and inner thought and feeling is the hallmark of Gilbertian comedy, and it is seen most readily in *Engaged*, Gilbert's prose comedy of 1877, in which the characters' motivations of greed and selfishness are completely at variance with their charitable demeanours. Minnie Symperson, the heroine, has all the outward trappings of the submissive, dutiful, rather foolish Victorian wife; but beneath this exterior lurks a powerful urge for dominance. She outlines her philosophy of marriage to her father: 'Papa, dear, I have thought the matter over very carefully in my little baby-noodle, and I have come to the conclusion – don't laugh at me, dear papa – that it is my duty – my duty – to fall in with Cheviot's views in everything before marriage, and Cheviot's duty to fall into my view in everything after marriage.' The hero, Cheviot Hill, is 'cursed with a strange amatory disposition' which causes him to flirt with every woman he meets. He expresses his fidelity to women with an ardour that has the semblance of sincerity, but this is continually undercut by new attraction to whatever female form passes into view. Even on his wedding day, he cannot resist flirting with his future wife's maid. Symperson, Minnie's father, stands to gain one thousand pounds by his daughter's marriage to Cheviot. He also stands to inherit the same amount if Cheviot dies. The scene in which Cheviot reminds him of this is similar to that in *The Mikado* where Ko-Ko persuades Nanki-Poo to be executed:

CHEVIOT: There is another contingency on which you come into the money. My death.

SYMPERSON: To be sure! I never thought of that! And, as you say, a man can die but once.

CHEVIOT: I beg your pardon. I didn't say anything of the kind – you said it; but it's true, for all that.

SYMPERSON: I'm very sorry; but, of course, if you have made up your mind to it.

CHEVIOT: Why, when a man's lost everything, what has he to live for?

SYMPERSON: True, true. Nothing whatever. Still –

CHEVIOT: His money gone, his credit gone, the three girls he's engaged to gone.

SYMPERSON: I cannot deny it. It is a hopeless situation. Hopeless, quite hopeless.

CHEVIOT: His happiness wrecked, his hopes blighted; the three trees upon which the fruit of his heart was growing – all cut down. What is left but suicide?

SYMPERSON: True, true! You're quite right. Farewell (*going*).

CHEVIOT: Symperson, you seem to think I want to kill myself. I don't want to do anything of the kind. I'd much rather live – upon my soul I would – if I could think of any reason for living. Symperson, can't you think of something to check the heroic impulse which

is at this moment urging me to a tremendous act of
self-destruction?

SYMPERSON: Something! Of course I can! Say that you
throw yourself into the Serpentine – which is handy.
Well, it's an easy way of going out of the world, I'm
told – rather pleasant than otherwise, I believe –
quite an agreeable sensation, I'm given to understand.
But you – you get wet through; and your – your
clothes are absolutely ruined!

CHEVIOT: (*mournfully*) For that matter, I could take off
my clothes before I went in.

SYMPERSON: True, so you could. I never thought of
that. You could take them off before you go in –
there's no reason why you shouldn't, if you do it in
the dark – and that objection falls to the ground.
Cheviot, my lion-hearted boy, it's impossible to resist
your arguments, they are absolutely convincing.
(*Shakes his hand. Exit.*)

In both scenes, the characters' selfish motives overrule
sympathy for the death of a fellow human being.

In *Engaged* and in the operas, Gilbert views mankind
with cynicism: no matter how severe the rules of social
conduct, people will circumvent them in order to satisfy
their motives of selfishness and self-preservation.

In *The Mikado*, Pooh-Bah is the character who most
completely epitomises the Gilbertian view of mankind.
Because all the officers of state of Titipu have resigned,
he has assumed multiple political positions, including
First Lord of the Treasury, Lord Chief Justice,
Commander-in-Chief, Lord High Admiral, Master of
the Buckhounds, Groom of the Back Stairs, Archbishop
of Titipu and Lord Mayor. In the scene in which Ko-Ko
consults him about his wedding expenses, Pooh-Bah

assumes each of these roles and their attitudes as skilfully as an actor changing masks:

> Of course, as First Lord of the Treasury, I could propose a special vote that would cover all expenses, if it were not that, as Leader of the Opposition, it would be my duty to resist it, tooth and nail. Or, as Paymaster-General, I could so cook the accounts that, as Lord High Auditor, I should never discover the fraud. But then, as Archbishop of Titipu, it would be my duty to denounce my dishonesty and give myself into my own custody as First Commissioner of Police.

The ludicrous aspect here is that it is the titles, and not Pooh-Bah's true feelings or opinions that dictate his utterances. Although this conformity to his social duties gives him the veneer of respectability, Pooh-Bah's real motivation is greed for money. As Pish-Tush points out, when he assumed the positions he also assumed all of the salaries associated with them, and he is only willing to provide help to others if he is bribed. As he says to Ko-Ko,

> I don't say that all these distinguished people couldn't be squared; but it is right to tell you that they wouldn't be sufficiently degraded in their own estimation unless they were insulted with a very considerable bribe.

The most potent satire in the Savoy Operas is not the mockery of particular institutions such as the law and the House of Lords, but the exposure of human hypocrisy in characters such as Pooh-Bah. Gilbert delights in showing the discrepancy between outer appearance and inner reality in human behaviour – especially when that reality is sordid and unpleasant. This preoccupation reflects the society in which he lived. As Walter Houghton points out in *The Victorian Frame of Mind*, the Victorians lived in an age when standards of conduct were high – in fact, 'too high for human nature'. Under the influence of Evangelical religious thought Victorians were expected to behave in accord with strict ideals of propriety, duty, sobriety and earnestness. Inevitably, there was a gap between these ideals and reality: 'As men were required to support Christianity by church attendance and active charity, and to accept the moral ideals of earnestness, enthusiasm, and sexual purity, the gap between profession and practice, or between profession and the genuine character, widened to an unusual extent.'[7] In his plays and operas, Gilbert shows an acute awareness of the conflict between the demands of society for conformity and the wishes and urges of the individual. In *The Mikado*, this is expressed in the conflict between the Mikado, who represents the demands of the state, and the ambitions of the other characters.

All the characters in *The Mikado* are hypocrites in the wide sense of the original meaning of the word, which in Greek means 'actor'. Nanki-Poo is a prince disguised as a wandering minstrel; Ko-Ko is a cheap tailor trying to play the role of public executioner; Pooh-Bah's outer respectability contrasts with his greed; and Katisha's ungainly form hides a tender interior. On top of these ironies of characterisation lies the further irony that the story is played out by English actors who don Japanese make-up and costumes only to behave in a perfectly English way. For the original audience, part of the delight of *The Mikado* came from the recognition of familiar performers dressed in Japanese costume – giving to the

Gilbert and Sullivan

opera the atmosphere of fancy dress party. Layer on
layer, mask on mask, this richness, together with its
superb construction and universal themes, make *The
Mikado* Gilbert and Sullivan's masterpiece and account
for its continuing appeal to audiences and performers.

4
A Victorian Looking-Glass: 'The Sorcerer' and 'H.M.S. Pinafore'

The Mikado illustrates all the important structural features of Gilbert and Sullivan opera. The dramatic tension created by the separation of lovers, the rapid and bewildering *peripetiae* of plot, and the subdivision of dramatic action into small units of dialogue and song are found in the other twelve full-length operas. The structural formality of the Savoy Operas is reminiscent of classical drama. The alternation of dialogue scenes in which issues are discussed and new courses of action planned with musical passages which comment on the action is very similar to the alteration of dialogue and choral passages in Greek comedy and tragedy. This similarity undoubtedly has its roots in Gilbert's classical education.

The other operas differ from *The Mikado* not in deviation from this form but in content. The major

71

difference is the degree to which elements drawn from contemporary British society are incorporated into the setting and plot. In *The Mikado*, Victorian England is hidden behind a Japanese facade; in earlier operas, this pretence does not exist. The six operas written from 1875 (*Trial by Jury*) to 1882 (*Iolanthe*) constitute a group that is homogeneous in style and approach. Their common feature is that they are set in Victorian England and satirise specific aspects of Victorian society. The general satiric approach is to combine everyday reality with fantasy: thus, in *The Pirates of Penzance* a Victorian Major-General and his daughters out for a seaside picnic meet a group of pirates; in *The Sorcerer*, an English village succumbs to a magical love-potion; in *Iolanthe*, the House of Lords clashes with fairyland. Often, the chief focus of satire is a single individual who represents a particular social or political institution: Sir Joseph Porter in *Pinafore* represents the civil service, Doctor Daly in *The Sorcerer* the clergy, Major-General Stanley the army, and the Lord Chancellor the law. The intrusion of this individual and his entourage into the fantasy world allows a comparison of his behaviour and the actions of the fantasy characters: frequently he is found wanting. For example, the Major-General's dishonesty contrasts with the gentlemanly conduct of the pirates.

Beneath their superficial topicality, however, these operas have much in common with *The Mikado*. Their major theme is the conflict between the individual and social law; but in these operas, real laws drawn from the moral and social codes of Victorian England substitute for the fictional laws of Titipu. One of the most easily identifiable social laws affecting characters in these operas is the law of social rank. In Act I of *The Mikado*, Ko-Ko tells the chorus that in his transformation from tailor to executioner he has been 'Wafted by a favouring gale/To a height that few can scale.' The image of vertical movement is significant, for it draws attention to the idea of social rank that permeates the operas. The notion of class is so universal in the Savoy Operas that it is best regarded as a fundamental principle of characterisation and plot. Characters represent different social classes: in *Iolanthe*, for example, the Earls Mountararat and Tolloller are aristocrats while the hero Strephon is a lowly shepherd. Many characters conduct themselves with conscious awareness of their social position: Pooh-Bah, for example, says 'I'm not in the habit of saying "how de do, little girls, how de do?" to anybody under the rank of a Stockbroker.' Like Ko-Ko, characters slide up and down the social scale. This may happen by their own efforts: the Judge in *Trial by Jury* has raised himself from an 'impecunious party' to 'as rich as the Gurneys'. More often, characters change their rank by intervention of fate as at the end of *The Gondoliers*, the Duke of Plaza-Toro's servant Luiz turns out to be the King of Barataria. Finally, rank is an impediment to love: in *Pinafore*, Ralph and Josephine are separated by the differences in their rank.

The preoccupation with social class in the characters and situations of the operas reflects its importance in Victorian society. In the 1870s, Henry James wrote: 'The essentially hierarchical plan of English society is the great and ever-present fact to the mind of a stranger; there is hardly a detail of life that does not in some degree betray it.'[1] Victorian society was divided into several clearly defined strata. At the top, just beneath royalty, was the aristocracy, which derived its prestige and power from hereditary titles and the ownership of large quantities of land. This class traditionally wielded great political power through its representation in important political positions, and also provided leadership in fashion and the arts. By the mid-nineteenth century, its dominance was threatened by the emergence of the middle class, whose expansion has been called 'the great phenomenon of nineteenth-century social history'.[2] The rise of the middle class was based on the Industrial Revolution which created wealth for manufacturers and businessmen of all sorts, and also on its Puritan ideals of hard work, thrift and self-advancement. Middle-class Victorians viewed the life of the aristocracy, which it perceived as revolving around hunting and fishing on country estates and parties in London town houses, as idle and corrupt. Below the middle class was the vast majority of the population who filled the rank and file of the working class: farmers, factory workers, servants, tradesmen and labourers. Within each of these broad classes there were sub-classes: in the middle class, for example, a physician ranked above a shopkeeper; in the lower class, a skilled craftsman ranked above a navvy.

The hierarchical nature of Victorian society is depicted in the drama of the period. Tom Robertson's *Caste* (1867) deals with the marriage of George D'Alroy, an aristocrat, and Esther Eccles, a dancer. George's interest in Esther is condemned by his mother the Marchioness and by his friend Hawtree, who sums up the prevailing attitude of the day:

> My dear Dal, all those marriages of people with common people are all very well in novels and in plays on the stage, because the real people don't exist, and have no relatives who exist, and no connections, and so no harm's done, and it's rather interesting to look at; but in real life with real relations, and real mothers,

and so forth, it's absolute bosh. It's worse – it's utter social and personal annihilation and damnation.

The same idea is expressed comically by Sam, Esther's father, when he says: 'People should stick to their own class. Life's a railway journey, and Mankind's a passenger – first class, second class, third class. Any person found riding in a superior class to that for which he has taken his ticket will be removed at the first station stopped at, according to the by-laws of the company.' In the Savoy Operas, these ideas are best depicted in the entrance of the Peers in *Iolanthe*. As they march round the stage in their robes and coronets, they sing:

> Bow, bow, ye lower middle classes!
> Bow, bow, ye tradesmen, bow, ye masses!
> Blow the trumpets, bang the brasses!
> Tantantara! Tzing! Boom!
> We are peers of highest station,
> Paragons of legislation,
> Pillars of the British Nation!

The command to 'Bow, bow' illustrates the Victorian notion of deference, or acknowledgement of one's superiors, a principle that governed every aspect of Victorian life. Pooh-Bah refers to the same idea when he says the decapitated head 'clearly knew/The deference due/To a man of pedigree.'

References to class distinction are found in all the operas, but in two – *The Sorcerer* and *H.M.S. Pinafore* – the idea of rank assumes central importance. A glance at the *Dramatis Personae* of *The Sorcerer* shows that all Victorian social classes are represented on stage. Sir Marmaduke Pointdextre, an 'elderly baronet', and Lady Sangazure, a 'Lady of Ancient Lineage' are representatives of the landowning nobility. The action of the opera takes place in the grounds of Sir Marmaduke's Elizabethan mansion and begins with the marriage of their children, Alexis Pointdextre and Aline Sangazure. This union, says Sir Marmaduke, 'realises my fondest wishes. Aline is rich, and she comes of a sufficiently old family, for she is the seven thousand and thirty seventh in direct descent from Helen of Troy.' The other characters are drawn from lower ranks: Dr Daly, the vicar, is respectably middle class; Mrs Partlet, the village pew-opener, is of the rural lower class; and John Wellington Wells, an urban intruder into the rustic world of the opera, is a tradesman ('I drop my H's – have through life'). Cavorting in the background is a chorus of common folk, the villagers of Ploverleigh.

The first section of the opera, up to the signing of the marriage contract by Alexis and Aline, introduces romantic attachments between these characters. Constance, Mrs Partlet's daughter, is in love with the vicar, who declares his intent to 'live and die a solitary bachelor'. Sir Marmaduke harbours a secret passion for Lady Sangazure. The mutual affection of these two characters is suppressed beneath a mask of propriety: when Sir Marmaduke enters, the stage direction is: 'Lady Sangazure and he exhibit signs of strong emotion at the sight of each other, which they endeavour to repress'.

After these relationships are established and Alexis and Aline have signed the contract, the action of the opera begins. Alexis reveals a plan by which he hopes to bring happiness to the whole village. Despite his aristocratic origins, he believes 'true happiness comes of true love, and true love should be independent of external influences', which include class distinction. Alexis expounds his ideas zealously:

Still I have made some converts to the principle, that
men and women should be coupled in matrimony
without distinction of rank. I have lectured on the
subject at Mechanics' Institutes, and the mechanics
were unanimous in favour of my views. I have preached
in workhouses, beershops, and Lunatic Asylums, and I
have been received with enthusiasm. I have addressed
navvies on the advantages that would accrue to them if
they married wealthy ladies of rank, and not a navvy
dissented!

The discrepancy between the earnest tone of this speech –
reminiscent of an itinerant preacher – and the comic
intrusion of the image of the Lunatic Asylum suggests
that even at this early stage in the opera Alexis is not to
be taken very seriously.

After recapitulating his principles in song, Alexis
introduces John Wellington Wells, a Family Sorcerer,
whom he has hired to dispense a love potion to the
villagers. The effects of the potion are described by
Wells: 'Whoever drinks of it loses consciousness for a
period, and on waking falls in love, as a matter of course,
with the first lady he meets who has also tasted it, and his
affection is at once returned.' Alexis is the first of a series
of heroes and heroines in the Savoy Operas who are
obsessed with an idea or opinion they attempt, invariably
unsuccessfully, to put into practice. In *Princess Ida*, the
title character is driven by the idea of female superiority,
and to that end she establishes a woman's university; in
The Gondoliers Marco and Giuseppe reform the monarchy
of Barataria in line with their republican principles. This
comic device is derived in part from Victorian farce, in
which eccentric characters obsessed with an idea are
frequently found. Comedy arises from the consequences

of trying to impose an unreasonable or irrational idea on a reluctant or hostile world. In Thomas Williams' *Pipkin's Rustic Retreat* (1866), for example, the main character is obsessed with the idea that country life is better than city life. He therefore moves his family from the comfort of their city home into a dilapidated country mansion; this proves comically disastrous to all.

Alexis' obsession with free love between the classes is expressed in a way that renders it free from any suggestion of impropriety. When he sings of 'the love that loves for love alone', he is not singing of 'free love', which was a Victorian euphemism for sexual promiscuity. Instead, Alexis' vision is that of wedded domestic bliss:

> What man for any other joy can thirst,
> Whose loving wife adores him duly?
> Want, misery and care may do their worst,
> If loving woman loves you truly.

One of the essential differences between Offenbach and Gilbert and Sullivan is apparent here. Offenbach would have used the device of the love potion to create all sorts of naughty adventures between characters, married or unmarried; Gilbert and Sullivan's potion comes with a guarantee that it will not offend. When Aline reacts to the potion with 'Alexis, many of the villagers are married people!', Mr Wells says, 'Madam, this philtre is compounded on the strictest principles. On married people it has no effect whatever.' Here Gilbert is jabbing at the Puritanical morality of middle-class Victorians – but he is also taking care to render his opera free from any indelicate suggestions that might cause those same Victorians to turn away from the box office.

At the end of Act I, the potion is delivered to the

villagers by means of a teapot: this is a clever juxtaposition of the supernatural with an item drawn from the everyday domestic world of the audience. A further irony is added by the fact that it is the respectable vicar, Dr Daly, who makes the tea and pours the cups from which the characters become intoxicated. As the tea is served, Mr Wells, Alexis and Aline sing:

> See – see – they drink –
> All thought unheeding,
> The tea-cups clink,
>   They are exceeding!
> Their hearts will melt
>   In half an hour –
> Then will be felt
>   The potion's power!

Act II depicts the farcical consequences of ingestion of the love potion. As a result of drinking the potion, each member of the pairs of lovers introduced in Act I is now aligned with a new, socially incompatible mate. Constance, for example, falls in love with the village Notary, who is described in terms of physical repugnance: 'dry and snuffy, deaf and slow,/Ill-tempered, weak, and poorly!/He's ugly, and absurdly dressed.' Lady Sangazure turns her attention from Sir Marmaduke to John Wellington Wells, who has not taken the potion. He repudiates her despite her promise that she will forswear her aristocratic manners – this includes the ludicrous threat to 'stick sunflowers in my hair'. Sir Marmaduke, meanwhile, has fallen for Mrs Partlet, who tells a stunned Alexis, 'I am aware that socially I am not everything that could be desired, nor am I blessed with an abundance of worldly goods, but I can at least confer on your estimable father the great and priceless dowry of a true, tender and lovin' 'art!' The climax of this menagerie of ill-assorted love occurs when Aline drinks the potion and accidentally falls in love with Dr Daly. When Alexis discovers them singing a love duet, he is enraged, and demands that John Wellington Wells reverse the spell immediately. The removal of the magic involves the death of either Alexis or Mr Wells, but as the sorcerer is considered 'the cause of all offending' he is asked to sacrifice his life. As a gong sounds, the charm is lifted, and the characters regroup with their proper partners:

> *All quit their present partners, and rejoin their old lovers. Sir Marmaduke leaves Mrs. Partlet, and goes to Lady Sangazure. Aline leaves Dr. Daly, and goes to Alexis. Dr. Daly leaves Aline, and goes to Constance. Notary leaves Constance and goes to Mrs. Partlet. All the chorus make a corresponding change.*

As Mr Wells disappears through the floor of the stage 'amid red fire', the characters celebrate the restoration of normality with a dance.

For its audience, the message of *The Sorcerer* is comforting. The demolition of class barriers by the potion leads to chaos and confusion, and a return to the stable world of rank is inevitable. The overall pattern of the opera is a movement from order into confusion and back to order again. The transition occurs when the characters drink the potion. As they 'stagger round the stage as if under the influence of a narcotic', they sing:

> Oh, marvellous illusion!
> Oh, terrible surprise!
> What is this strange confusion
> That veils my aching eyes?

> I must regain my senses,
> Restoring Reason's law,
> Or fearful inferences
> The company will draw!

As the characters 'fall insensible on the stage', the
threshold between the world of 'Reason's law' and that
of 'strange confusion' is crossed. When they awake in the
second act, it is to a world where social conventions do
not exist. At least, they do not *appear* to exist. We notice
that even in this section of the opera the characters
maintain a sense of decorum: when Alexis and Aline
notice that their parents are not among the slumbering
forms, John Wellington Wells tells them that he had
them 'taken home/And put to bed respectably!'

The second act begins at midnight, and the characters
are discovered asleep onstage. As they awaken, they fall
in love with one another; but the grotesque pairings that
result suggest that they have awakened not to reality but
to a dream. It is a dream not without pleasure for its
audience. Set against the background of Victorian social
conventions, the second act of the opera, in which
characters are free to pick and choose their mates without
regard for the established rules of social behaviour, is a
fantasy for an audience whose own amatory behaviour
was governed by the rules of class. This fantasy involves
the temporary suspension of these rules and the enactment
of forbidden ideas: a beautiful young girl falls in love
with an ugly old man, an aristocrat woos a plain but
cheerful commoner, a middle-aged vicar wins the love of
a young lady, and a dowager chases a tradesman.

An identical pattern of events occurs in Gilbert's poetic
comedy *The Palace of Truth* (1870). The first act of this
play introduces a group of characters chief amongst

whom is Prince Philamir, the 'bravest and most accomplished Prince in Christendom', who is betrothed to Princess Zeolide, daughter of Queen Altemire and King Phanor. We meet several characters of Phanor's court, such as the pedant Zoram. Zeolide appears to receive Philamir's love indifferently, and in order to discover whether she really loves him, Phanor decides that his entire court shall journey to the Palace of Truth:

> That palace is enchanted. Every one
> Who enters there is bound to speak the truth –
> The simple, unadulterated truth.
> To every question that is put to him
> He must return the unaffected truth.
> And strange to say, while publishing the truth
> He's no idea that he is doing so;
> And while he lets innumerable cats
> Out of unnumbered bags, he quite believes
> That all the while he's tightening the strings
> That keep them from a too censorious world.

In the second act, the characters arrive in the Palace of Truth, and are forced to speak the truth to each other. Under the influence of truth, the characters are shown to be the opposites of what we expect: the cold Zeolide loves Philamir passionately, Philamir turns out to be a heartless cad, Zoram is a charlatan, and King Phanor openly tells his wife all his marital indiscretions. As a result of revealing the truth, engagements are broken off, friendships are dissolved, and general discord and chaos results. As at the end of *The Sorcerer*, there is general relief at the end of the play when the characters leave the Palace and resume the normal conventions of social behaviour. One of the characters says simply, 'We shall get on much better' outside the palace than in it.

The common dramatic device of *The Palace of Truth* and *The Sorcerer* is the use of magic temporarily to suspend the accepted rules of social conduct. In each play, the excursion away from social convention ends with a safe arrival back in the normal world. In *The Sorcerer*, the collapse of the fantasy is not unexpected, for the central object of satire in the opera is its promoter, Alexis. In Act I, his scheme is presented in a humorous way reminiscent of the eccentric characters of farce; in the second act, he becomes a less attractive character. He demands that Aline drink the potion to solidify her love for him, and she quite rightly interprets this as mistrust. He then assaults her in song: 'If such thy love, oh, shame!/Call it by other name – It is not love!' In this scene, Alexis' loss of perspective changes him from a character who is merely eccentric to a fanatic. Later on, he is shocked when his father declares his intention to marry Mrs Partlet: 'My dear father, this is not altogether what I expected. I am certainly taken somewhat by surprise . . . (*aside to Aline*). It is not quite what I could have wished.' It is all right for the common folk to marry without regard to rank, but when it comes to one's own father, that is a different matter. Alexis thus turns out to be a hypocrite, and his own distaste for the new world he creates makes its demise inevitable.

Alexis' double standards make him the prototype of Sir Joseph Porter in *H.M.S. Pinafore*. This opera, written the year after *Sorcerer*, is Gilbert and Sullivan's most thorough treatment of the topic of class distinction. As in the other operas, dramatic tension is built on the separation of two lovers. Ralph Rackstraw, a sailor on *H.M.S. Pinafore*, is in love with Josephine, his captain's daughter, but they cannot marry because of the difference in their social rank. Their union is blocked by Captain Corcoran, Josephine's father, and Sir Joseph Porter, the First Lord of the Admiralty, himself a rival for Josephine's hand. This stituation is mirrored in a subplot concerning the mutual admiration of the Captain and Little Buttercup, a Portsmouth bumboat woman, who are also prevented from marrying by the difference in their class.

The opera is a vivid tableau of the hierarchical nature of Victorian society. The stratification of the crew of the ship is a microscopic version of Victorian society as a whole: as Sir Joseph says to the Captain, 'an accident of birth has placed you above them and them below you'. Characters and events in the opera are described using images of vertical separation. Ralph is 'the lowliest tar that sails the water'; Josephine is 'highly born'. When Ralph describes his love for Josephine to his mates, the Bo'sun's instinctive response is to say, 'Ah, my poor lad, you've climbed too high'; when Josephine tells her father of her love for Ralph, she speaks of 'the depth to which I have stooped'. The imagery used by Ralph when he declares his love to Josephine is identical: 'wafted one moment into blazing day, by mocking hope – plunged the next into the Cimmerian darkness of tangible despair.' The Captain is 'rich and lofty', Buttercup 'poor and lowly'. The repetition of this image demonstrates the importance of the notion of vertical separation of people in the opera and in Victorian society.

The rustic setting of *The Sorcerer* is inherited from pastoral opera. *H.M.S. Pinafore* has roots in a different theatrical tradition, nautical melodrama. Early in the nineteenth century, writers of melodrama found ready material in the exploits of the British Navy. One of the most popular nautical dramas was Douglas Jerrold's

1. William Schwenck Gilbert, comic poet and librettist, 1836-1911. © National Portrait Gallery.

2. Arthur Seymour Sullivan, composer, 1842-1900. © National Portrait Gallery.

3. The Savoy Theatre, London, shortly after its opening in 1881. Onstage is a scene from Act I of *Patience*. Note the picture frame effect of the proscenium arch.

4. Contemporary engraving of the incantation scene from Act I of the original production of *The Sorcerer*, 1878.

5. *HMS Pinafore* revived at the Savoy in 1908. The 70-year old Gilbert supervised a series of revivals of the operas at the Savoy from 1906-1908, and photographs of these productions demonstrate the almost cinematic realism of design which dominated Gilbert's productions.

6. *HMS Pinafore*, Savoy 1908.

7. Contemporary engraving of scenes from the original production of *The Pirates of Penzance*, 1880.

8. Frederic titillates the daughters of Major-General Stanley, who have doffed not only their shoes and stockings but also their dresses in the 1985 Stratford Festival of Canada production of *The Pirates of Penzance*.
Jeff Hyslop as Frederic with (bottom left clockwise): Aggie Cekuta Elliott, Karen Skidmore, Wendy Abbott, Ruth Nichol, Lyndsay Richardson, Karen Wood, Marion Adler, Allison Grant.

9. The Fairy Queen bears an uncanny resemblance to Queen Victoria in the Stratford Festival of Canada production of *Iolanthe*, 1984.
Maureen Forrester as the Fairy Queen, Douglas Chamberlain as Earl Tolloller, Karen Wood as Fleta, Karen Skidmore as Leila, Eric Donkin as the Lord Chancellor, Allison Grant as Celia, Stephen Beamish as Earl Mountararat.

10. *The Mikado*, Savoy, 1908. Act I Finale.

11. *The Mikado*, Savoy, 1908. Act II. Henry Lytton, later to play the 'Grossmith' roles, here plays the Mikado.

12. Richard McMillan as Pooh-Bah with the male chorus in the 1983 Stratford Festival production of *The Mikado* which was presented at the reopening of the Old Vic Theatre in London in November 1983.

13. *The Yeomen of the Guard*, Savoy, 1906.

14. Peter Goffin's 1939 set for the D'Oyly Carte production of *Yeomen*. Comparison with previous plate shows the trend away from prictorial realism.

15. Contemporary engraving of Queen Victoria watching the command performance of *The Gondoliers* at Windsor Castle, March 1891.

16. A touch of Gilbertian sadism: Inez (Jean Stilwell) confesses from the rack in the final scene of the Stratford Festival production of *The Gondoliers*, 1983.

Black Ey'd Susan (1829), a play which typifies the form. Jerrold's play, set in the seaside village of Deal, Kent, recounts the adventures of a sailor-hero named William who speaks an incomprehensible nautical jargon: 'I can feel one tear standing in either eye like a marine at each gang-way; but come, let's send them below. (*Wipes his eyes.*)' He is a paragon of sailorly virtue: 'The trimmest sailor as ever handles rope; the first on his watch, the last to leave the deck; . . . from reefing a main top-sail to stowing a netting, give me taut Bill afore any able seaman in his Majesty's fleet.' When William strikes his Captain – who has drunkenly assaulted William's love Susan – he is sentenced to death, but in the last seconds of the play he is reprieved by the surprise revelation that his discharge orders from the navy had been written prior to the assault, so he is no longer subject to naval law.

William is the archetype of the Jolly Jack Tar, or sailor-hero, who is a superhuman blend of compassion, sensitivity, bravery, humour and patriotism. This figure was one of the most enduring of the nineteenth-century stage and even appeared in plays with no overt nautical element.

H.M.S. Pinafore is a direct descendant of nautical melodrama. The scene is the quarterdeck of *H.M.S. Pinafore*: in the background is the familiar harbour of Portsmouth, and we are welcomed on board by a crew of sailors who are 'sober men and true/And attentive to our duty.' Ralph speaks using the same sailorly metaphors as William: he describes Josephine as 'the figurehead of my ship of life – the bright beacon that guides me into my port of happiness.' Like William, Ralph finds himself in conflict with his commanding officer. The plot of the opera has a remarkable structural similarity to the play, with a last-minute reprieval of the hero by surprise revelation. The difference is that in *Pinafore* the conclusion is farcical: Ralph turns out to be the Captain, and the Captain, Ralph.

This ending is worthy of John Maddison Morton, and it gives *Pinafore* the touch of parody. The parody is mixed with sincere patriotic sentiment inherited from earlier melodrama. The persistence of nautical drama as a popular form over the fifty-year time span that separates *Susan* from *Pinafore* can be explained by the patriotic appeal of the form. During the mid-nineteenth century the British Navy's contribution to the expansion and protection of the British Empire made it the symbolic focus of national pride. As James Morris says, 'The British Navy was recognised as the ultimate arbiter of the world's affairs'.[3] At the time when *Pinafore* was written, Victoria had been named Empress of India, and the empire was rushing to its climax. The spirit of the era is easily found in the opera:

> He is an Englishman!
>   For he himself has said it,
>   And it's greatly to his credit,
> That he is an Englishman!
> For he might have been a Roosian,
> A French, or Turk, or Proosian,
> Or perhaps Italian!
> But in spite of all temptations,
> To belong to other nations,
>   He remains an Englishman!

It is easy to see why this piece quickly became a standard part of the repertoire of every colonial band from Bombay to Bermuda.

In the half-century that separates *Black Ey'd Susan* from *Pinafore*, the London theatre audience had changed from primarily working class to a mixed audience dominated by the middle class. Early-nineteenth-century melodramas such as *Black Ey'd Susan* reflected the aspirations of their audience. The political attitude of melodrama was egalitarian. Discarding the traditional view of human value based on rank or wealth, melodrama chose as its heroes examples of 'nature's gentlemen' – lower-class citizens such as sailors and labourers who despite their lowly rank were innately more virtuous than their superiors. Their adventures involved struggles against villains from the higher classes – wicked aristocrats, greedy factory owners, heartless landowners, and so on. As Michael Booth observes: 'Much melodrama, particularly the domestic, is permeated with class hatred and darkened by a grim vision of a wealthy, authoritarian, repressive upper class tyrannizing over a poor suffering proletariat.'[4]

H.M.S. Pinafore was written for a largely middle-class audience, but it retains the vestiges of the political spirit of its ancestors. The main impediment to Ralph's love for Josephine is rank, but Ralph cannot understand this: 'But it's a strange anomaly, that the daughter of a man who hails from the quarter-deck may not love another who lays out on the fore-yard arm. For a man is but a man, whether he hoists his flag at the main-truck or his slacks on the main-deck.' Encouraged by Sir Joseph's pronouncements on human equality, he decides to speak to Josephine: 'Is not my love as good as another's? Is not my heart as true as another's? Have I not hands and eyes and ears and limbs like another?' Ralph's comrades share his ideals. The Glee sung in the first act has the rebellious spirit of earlier melodrama:

A British tar is a soaring soul,
  As free as a mountain bird,
His energetic fist should be ready to resist
  A dictatorial word. . . .
His eyes should flash with an inborn fire,
  His brow with scorn be wrung;
He never should bow down to a domineering frown,
  Or the tang of a tyrant tongue.

There is a subtle change here. The object of the British sailors' scorn is not the upper class, but dictators and tyrants, suggesting the struggle is not an internal one pitting class against class but an external one against foreign enemies. This shift in attitude reflects the imperialist ambitions of the British people in the second half of the nineteenth century – ambitions which shifted attention away from domestic conflict to the excitement of empire-building.

Several of the other characters oppose Ralph's principles of equality. Captain Corcoran at first appears to be an enlightened officer: although 'related to a peer', he treats his crew with politeness. When Josephine reveals her love for Ralph, his true nature is revealed. Although he says 'I attach little value to rank or wealth', he adds 'the line must be drawn somewhere'. His insistence that Josephine marry Sir Joseph – hardly an attractive prospect for any woman – is cruel, especially since it is motivated by his own selfish strivings up the social scale. In Act II, when it appears Josephine has agreed to the match, the Captain utters his most characteristic statement: 'At last my fond hopes are to be crowned. My only daughter is to be the bride of a Cabinet Minister. The prospect is Elysian.' Captain Corcoran is reminiscent of Symperson in *Engaged* who urges the match between his daughter Minnie and Cheviot Hill because he stands to gain a thousand-pound annuity by it.

Captain Corcoran's objections to the marriage of his daughter to Ralph are understandable. The relentless opposition of Dick Deadeye to Ralph's plans is less comprehensible because as a fellow crew member he is of the same social class as the hero. Deadeye's function in the melodrama is as the villain: he thwarts the elopement of the lovers by informing the Captain of their flight. Like other villains in the Savoy Operas, he is physically unattractive and shunned by the other characters: 'I'm ugly, and they hate me for it, for you all hate me, don't you?' Nobody pays much attention to him, for 'From such a face and form as mine, the noblest sentiments sound like the black utterances of a depraved imagination.' The irony is that he is the spokesman for the most practical and realistic attitudes in the opera. He rejects the egalitarianism of both Ralph and Sir Joseph: 'You're on a wrong tack, and so is he. When people have to obey other people's orders, equality is out of the question.' When he appears at the end of the first act, it is to remind the characters of the violation of rank that Ralph and Josephine are committing:

> Forbear, nor carry out the scheme you've planned;
> She is a lady – you a foremast hand!
> Remember, she's your gallant Captain's daughter,
> And you the meanest slave that crawls the water!

At the heart of the opera, then, is a philosophical conflict between Ralph's view of human equality and the other character's assertions of the importance of rank. This conflict is represented in Josephine, who is caught between her love for Ralph and duty to her father. Initially she announces that she will follow the path of duty: 'But fear not, father, I have a heart, and therefore I love; but I am your daughter, and therefore I am proud. Though I carry my love with me to the tomb, he shall never, never, know it.' When confronted by Ralph, she maintains a mask of propriety but her asides reveal her true feelings: 'Sir, this audacity! *(Aside.)* Oh, my heart, my beating heart! *(Aloud.)* This unwarrantable presumption on the part of a common sailor! *(Aside.)* Common! oh, the irony of the word!' The two aspects of Josephine's personality are expressed musically in the duet that follows this scene, where the musical styles of the verses change according to whether Josephine is speaking to Ralph or uttering her real feelings. The first verse, 'Refrain, audacious tar' is strident, almost military; the second, melodious and tender.

When Ralph threatens suicide, Josephine reveals her true feelings to him and agrees to elope with him that night. Even after this decision, she has doubts expressed in her second aria, which opens with the admission that 'My guilty heart is quaking!' This song is filled with vivid images that contrast the middle-class world of the Captain with lower-class life. 'Papa's luxurious home', for example, is 'hung with ancestral armour and old brasses', while in Ralph's home she expects to find 'one cracked looking-glass to see your face in,/And dinner served up in a pudding basin!' Despite her doubts, Josephine decides to marry Ralph when Sir Joseph assures her that it is his opinion that 'Love is a platform upon which all ranks meet'. The irony is that Sir Joseph thinks that he has persuaded her to marry him.

Sir Joseph is Ralph's rival, but for most of the opera his actions unwittingly promote the relationship between the young lovers. During his first appearance in the opera, his statements about human equality encourage Ralph to declare his love to Josephine. Sir Joseph's brand of egalitarianism is not based like Ralph's on early-nineteenth-century democratic ideals but on the mid-Victorian concept of the self-made man. Although the rigid social hierarchy of Victorian England remained intact for the whole century, by 1850 its foundations were being eroded by the widespread belief that it was the right of every Britain to raise his social position as best he could. This outlook is seen in a speech in 1850 by Lord Palmerston:

> We have shown the example of a nation in which every class of society accepts with cheerfulness the lot which providence has assigned to it; while at the same time each individual of each class is constantly trying to raise himself in the social scale, not by violence and illegality, but by persevering good conduct and by the steady and energetic exertion of the moral and intellectual faculties with which his creator has endowed him.[5]

For the lower classes, social improvement could be attained by education, hard work and independence; for the middle classes, by the acquisition of wealth and property and by making the right connections (such as marrying your daughter to a Cabinet Minister). The pressure to improve oneself permeated every aspect of Victorian life and literature: as one Victorian put it: 'To push on, to climb vigorously on the slippery slopes of the social ladder, to raise ourselves one step or more out of the rank of life in such we were born, is now converted into a duty.'[6] One of the most successful books of the period was Samuel Smiles' *Self-Help* published in 1859; it sold over a quarter of a million copies by 1905. This handbook to success suggested that by industry, determination and thrift any man could raise himself to the top of the social ladder.[7]

Sir Joseph Porter is the epitome of the Victorian self-made man. His autobiographical song tells the story of his rise from a mere office boy to 'ruler of the Queen's Navee'. Each verse represents a separate step up the social scale. Beginning as office boy to an attorney's firm, he 'cleaned the windows', 'swept the floor', and 'polished up the handle of the big front door' – activities which illustrate the credo of selfless hard work. In the second verse, he becomes a 'junior clerk' who serves writs with a 'smile so bland' and copies letters 'in a big round hand'. The first activity suggests an oily obsequiousness reminiscent of Uriah Heep; the second, a mindless attention to form without regard for content. As the song progresses, we sense Gilbert's contempt for Sir Joseph: the overall impression gained is that in order to rise in the world, it is not inner qualities but outer appearance that is important. This is confirmed in the next verse, where Sir Joseph tells us he wore 'clean collars and a brand new suit' for his law examination. The implication is that passing an examination does not require intelligence, but it does require clean clothes. In the next two verses, Sir Joseph reaches the top: he becomes a partner in a law firm and is elected to Parliament. This goal is achieved not by merit but by the use of wealth to purchase a 'pocket borough' (parliamentary seat belonging to a landowner who could use it as a gift or sell it). The same mindless behaviour continues in Parliament: 'I always voted at my party's call,/And I never thought of thinking for myself at all!' The final reward of this voyage of conformity is that Sir Joseph is appointed First Lord of the Admiralty, a position for which he has no qualifications whatsoever – as he admits: 'And that junior partnership I ween/Was the only ship I ever had seen.' For the original audience, the satire was sharpened by the knowledge that the First Lord of the Admiralty in Disraeli's government was W. H. Smith, a landlubber who had risen to prominence from a seller of newspapers in railway stations.

Sir Joseph is a symbol, albeit a satirical one, of the possibilities of erasing class barriers. At first, his attitudes seem democratic. He berates Captain Corcoran for not treating his crew with courtesy, and he issues the sailors a song 'designed to encourage independence of thought and action in the lower branches of the service, and to teach the principle that a British sailor is any man's equal, excepting mine'. The last two words reveal his true attitude. In the second Act, Captain Corcoran tells Sir Joseph that his daughter's reticence is based on her awareness of the differences in their rank. Sir Joseph approaches Josephine and tells her 'Madam, I desire to convey to you officially my opinion that love is a platform upon which all ranks meet.' When at the end of the opera he discovers Josephine is really the daughter of a common sailor, he rejects her. The Captain protests that 'Love levels all ranks', but Sir Joseph says 'It does to a considerable extent, but it does not level them as much as that.' That statement is a succinct expression of the Victorian double standard which arose out of the conflict between the notion of class and the idea of self-advancement. While Victorians recognised the principle of 'removable inequalities', it was difficult to apply it in practice: to allow one's daughter to marry beneath her station or to befriend persons of a different rank required a greater effort of self-will than most Victorians could provide. Gilbert exposes this hypocrisy in the character of Sir Joseph.

Sir Joseph thus turns out to be as strong a pillar of the laws of class as anybody else. In the final scene of the opera, the class system is demolished. When Captain Corcoran discovers the elopement of the lovers and Sir Joseph learns that Ralph is his rival, an impasse in the action is reached. Ralph is banished to a dungeon; but at this moment, with the lovers separated and the forces of class apparently victorious, Little Buttercup steps forward with a revelation that reverses the situation. She reveals that she nursed Captain Corcoran and Ralph in infancy, and mixed them up. Ralph is actually the Captain, and the Captain Ralph. This news instantly resolves the dilemma of the plot: Josephine, now the daughter of a common sailor, is socially compatible with Ralph; she is incompatible with Sir Joseph, who relinquishes her. The Captain is free to marry Buttercup. The curtain falls amidst the celebration of the triple mating of Ralph and Josephine, Captain Corcoran and Buttercup, and Sir Joseph and his cousin Hebe.

The ludicrous aspect of the opera's ending is the calm acceptance with which the characters react to these reversals of social situation. The events at the end of the opera occur with such rapidity that the fact that the new arrangement still makes Ralph and Josephine incompatible (she is now lowly, he lofty) is overlooked. Indeed, the final scene has an aura of magic which is reinforced by the appearance of Ralph and the Captain in different costumes despite their being offstage during Buttercup's revelations. These changes of costume symbolise the characters' new social status and the corresponding change of the other characters' attitudes to them. As soon as he is shown to be a common sailor, the Captain is treated like one; similarly, Ralph begins to order people around. The other characters disregard the idea that Captain Corcoran and Ralph are still the same *people* as they were five minutes earlier; their value as individuals is changed simply as a result of their new social labels. Yet their new value depends on nothing other than an arbitrary assignation of class, and it is this arbitrariness which demonstrates the meaninglessness of the class system.

This ending differs from *The Sorcerer*, where a wave of the magic wand re-establishes the normal world. *Pinafore* ends with a superficial return to normality in the reprise of 'For he is an Englishman'. However, this reiteration of patriotic sentiment does not disguise the uncertainty left by the last scene of the opera, where Gilbert challenges the Victorians' most fundamental attitudes to each other.

5
Through the Looking-Glass: 'The Pirates of Penzance' and 'Patience'

When the curtain rose for the first time on Act I of *The Pirates of Penzance*, the scene was immediately familiar to the audience:

> *Scene – A rocky sea-shore on the coast of Cornwall. In the distance is a calm sea, on which a schooner is lying at anchor. As the curtain rises groups of pirates are discovered – some drinking, some playing cards. Samuel, the Pirate Lieutenant, is going from one group to another, filling the cups from a flask.*

The scenery, costumes, characters and onstage activity instantly reminded the onlookers of melodrama; indeed, the piece was billed as 'A New and Original Melo-Dramatic Opera'. *The Pirates of Penzance* has the outward appearance of a true 'blood and thunder' melodrama: there is a pirate band that attacks a bevy of beautiful maidens, a setting ('A ruined chapel by moonlight') that invokes suspense and terror, and a patriotic tableau at the end of Act I when the Major-General brandishes the Union Jack against the skull and crossbones. This latter device alludes to melodramas such as *The White Swan* where the hero and heroine are protected from the clutches of the villain by wrapping themselves in the Union Jack.[1]

H.M.S. Pinafore and *The Pirates of Penzance* have several features in common: they are both inspired by melodrama and they are constructed according to the romantic opera plan of dialogue alternating with songs. The fundamental problem of this plan is the integration of musical numbers into the dramatic action of the opera. Earlier writers of English opera in the nineteenth century failed to solve this problem, so that the operas had a peculiar stop-and-go quality, with the dramatic action interrupted at regular intervals by songs with tenuous musical or thematic relevance to the story. One of the chief differences between *H.M.S. Pinafore* and *The Pirates of Penzance* is that in the latter opera the songs are integrated into the dramatic action. In *Pinafore*, the musical numbers are set pieces which interrupt rather than carry forward the story. This is particularly true of the first act, where the first seven musical numbers are expository and descriptive and do little to move the action ahead. The emphasis on description is shown by the number of songs beginning in the first person: 'We sail the ocean blue', 'I'm called Little Buttercup', 'I am the Captain of the *Pinafore*', and 'I am the monarch of the sea'. It is not until the scene at the end of the act where Ralph threatens suicide that dramatic action is expressed musically. In the second act, much more of the action is set to music, but even here the flow of events is interrupted by Josephine's lengthy musical soliloquy.

The solution to this problem of musical and dramatic unity involves a shift in focus of the songs from the audience to the other characters. In *The Pirates of Penzance*, the characters generally sing to *one another* rather than to the audience or to the world in general. This difference is shown by comparing the songs which introduce the heroine in each opera. Josephine appears on stage alone and sings:

> Sorry her lot who loves too well,
> Heavy the heart that hopes but vainly,
> Sad are the sighs that own the spell,
> Uttered by eyes that speak too plainly.

Although this song fits the situation of Josephine's love for Ralph, the words and sentiment are not specific. The song could easily be transplanted to another opera with the same situation or to the concert stage where it could stand on its own. In *Pirates*, Mabel enters a stage filled with other characters, and she first addresses her sisters:

> Oh, sisters, deaf to pity's name,
> For shame!
> It's true that he has gone astray,
> But pray . . .

The emphasis is not on communication of information to the audience but on Mabel's interaction with the other characters. Her introductory song is aimed directly at Frederic:

> Poor wandering one!
> Though thou hast surely strayed,
> Take heart of grace,
> Thy steps retrace,
> Poor wandering one!

Although these words are still rather non-specific, the use of the second person gives a sharper focus than Josephine's song. Mabel is singing to a person, not to the open air; her song attempts to influence the feelings of another character.

In addition, much more of the dramatic action of *The Pirates* is set to music. The action of the central section of the first act is carried forward by a series of brilliant musical numbers. The momentum begins with the entrance of the female chorus, is maintained by Mabel's waltz-song and the 'Chattering chorus', and builds to a climax when the girls are captured by the pirates. This moment is beautifully timed: just as the girls are about to depart, they are interrupted in mid-sentence:

GIRLS: Too late!
PIRATES: Ha! Ha!
GIRLS: Too late!
PIRATES: Ha! Ha!

The greater sophistication of *The Pirates* is also seen in the handling of the choruses. In *Pinafore*, the sailors and the 'sisters, cousins, and aunts' of Sir Joseph are little more than stage scenery. The little interaction between male and female choruses is friendly: the sailors welcome the ladies on board the ship 'most politely'. In *Pirates*, the choruses have a larger role in the action and indulge in their own conflict. The female chorus, led by Mabel's sisters Edith and Kate, acts as commentator on the propriety of the other characters' behaviour. When their father appears in a dressing gown in the second act, the girls rush on to ask 'Why does father leave his rest/At such a time of night as this, so very incompletely dressed?' In the first act, the pirates capture the girls and declare their intention to marry them against their will. The finale to this act depicts the Major-General's extrication of his daughters from this predicament through arousing the pirate's sympathy by declaring that he is an orphan. At the end of the opera, the pirates are revealed to be noblemen, and the Major-General distributes his daughters to them. The union of male and female choruses at the end of the opera parallels the marriage of the main characters and supports the mood of celebration.

Following the tradition of melodrama, in *Pinafore* the big secret about the hero's true identity is withheld until the final moments of the opera. In *The Pirates* there is a clever reversal of this pattern: Ruth reveals Frederic's origins in the second musical number. The central action on the opera depends not on the revelation of Frederic's true identity but on a discovery which reverses his fortunes. In Act I, Frederic, who was mistakenly apprenticed to a band of pirates as a boy, attains his twenty-first birthday and is freed from his indentures to the pirates. He bids farewell to his pirate comrades and falls in love with Mabel, the daughter of Major-General Stanley. In the second act, Frederic discovers that he was born on 29 February in leap year, and although he has lived twenty-one years, by birthdays he is only five years old. He is still technically an apprentice to the pirates, and actuated by his sense of duty he returns to them. The humour lies in the disparity between the triviality of Frederic's birthday and the importance assigned to it.

Gilbert is here mocking the arbitrary and illogical discoveries and reversals of melodrama.

In *Pinafore*, the separation of lovers is caused by the external force of class distinction. One of the interesting and unconventional aspects of *The Pirates* is that the hero and heroine are forced apart by the hero's personality. As the subtitle of the opera indicates, Frederic is the 'slave of duty', and his actions are directed by his conscience. When the daughters of Major-General Stanley remove their shoes to go for a paddle in the sea, he is compelled by 'bounden duty' to reveal himself lest they embarrass themselves. In the second act, he decides to return to the pirate band and rejects Mabel despite her entreaties:

MABEL: Stay, Frederic, stay!
FRED: Nay, Mabel, nay!
MABEL: They have no claim –
FRED: But Duty's name!
      The thought my soul appals,
      But when stern Duty calls,
      I must obey.

To audiences of the twentieth century, Frederic's behaviour is simply amusing. For Victorians, amusement was accompanied by recognition of a parody of the most extreme aspects of their own moral code. If there is anything that is universally connoted by the word 'Victorian', it is an image of moral rectitude. This image arises from the Evangelical religious thinking of the nineteenth century which held that to be a Christian it was insufficient merely to observe the doctrines and forms of the Church. You had to live every moment of life with a view to obtaining a place in heaven; this necessitated a strict code of behaviour based on frugality, sobriety, hard work, chastity, self-denial and a selfless devotion to duty. The human soul is precariously balanced between the forces of good and evil, and so the code required constant self-discipline. Any lapse of vigilance might lead you to succumb to worldly temptation, but if you lived according to these principles, you would reap a double reward. Not only would you gain a place in heaven, but you would achieve 'respectability', the Victorian middle-class nirvana which implied success and social acceptance.[2]

These ideas were disseminated on a popular level by such writers as Samuel Smiles who from 1859 to 1889 produced a series of books whose titles are a catalogue of Victorian virtues: *Self Help*, *Character*, *Thrift* and *Duty*.[3] These books are extended sermons illustrating the value of self-sacrifice, thrift, honesty, duty, patience and courage through examples of famous men and women from classical and modern history and literature. Smiles' intention was to teach young men that 'their happiness and well being in after life depended upon . . . their diligent self-culture, self-discipline, and self-control; and above all, upon the honest and upright performance of individual duty, which constitutes the glory of manly character.' The attitude of these books is indicated by Smiles' condemnation of 'constant giggling', which he interprets as 'a sure sign of a shallow mind'.

Smiles' *Duty*, ironically enough, appeared in the same year as *The Pirates of Penzance*. The opening sentence, 'Man does not live for himself alone', is the gist of a four-hundred page dissertation on the theme of 'obedience to duty at all costs and risks, is the very essence of the highest civilised life'. Smiles' view of human nature is simple. There is 'a strife between a higher and a lower nature within us – of spirit warring against flesh – of good striving for the mastery over evil'. The exercise of conscience through the performance of duty frees man from 'subjection to the lower parts of our nature'. Without duty, civilisation would collapse and man would be a beast. Duty is everywhere: 'First, there is the pervading, abiding sense of duty to God. Then follow others: – Duty to one's family; duty to our neighbours; duty of masters to servants, and of servants to masters; duty to our fellow-creatures; duty to the state, which has also its duty to perform to the citizen.' The great bulk of *Duty* is taken up with examples of duty which range from Florence Nightingale to a sheepdog who dies while dutifully driving a flock of sheep from Cumberland to Liverpool.

The moral attitudes of the Victorian period were embodied in its drama, particularly in melodrama which viewed the world in terms of a battle between good and evil. The heroes of Victorian plays are exaggerated projections of Victorian ideals of behaviour: their actions are motivated by self-sacrifice, patriotism and duty. The moral earnestness of serious drama at the time of writing of *The Pirates of Penzance* is seen in James Albery's *Duty* which was presented at the Prince of Wales' Theatre in 1879. This play transforms the principles of Smiles into drama. The hero learns to his horror that his dead father has left behind a mistress and an illegitimate child. Acting on the basis of loyalty to the memory of his father, the hero pretends that the mistress and child are his own. The father's reputation is saved, but the hero ruins his own name and causes grief for his own fiancee and mother.

The Pirates of Penzance is a burlesque of the moral attitudes epitomised by Albery's play. Frederic's charge to the female chorus summarises the Victorian view of the world:

> Oh, is there not one maiden breast
> Which does not feel the moral beauty
> Of making worldly interest
> Subordinate to sense of duty?

To most Victorians, the choice between 'worldly interest' and 'sense of duty' was the central dilemma of life. For Smiles and the hero of Albery's play, the answer was to follow the path of duty. In the character of Frederic, Gilbert mocks the intellectual and emotional sterility of this choice. Frederic is completely governed by his sense of duty, so that his behaviour in any situation is automatic and does not permit feeling or logic. As a result, most of his actions are completely illogical when viewed from the perspective of common sense. Although he was apprenticed to the pirates erroneously, he remained with them for twenty-one years out of duty to them. Duty has an almost magical power. He recognises the absurdity of the revelation that his birthday is in leap year, but the Pirate King and Ruth have merely to mention the word to persuade him to rejoin their band:

RUTH: We insist on nothing: we content ourselves with pointing out to you *your duty*.

KING: Your duty!

FREDERIC: *(after a pause.)* Well, you have appealed to my sense of duty, and my duty is only too clear. I abhor your infamous calling; I shudder at the thought that I have ever been mixed up with it; but duty is before all – at any price I will do my duty.

Frederic's obsession with duty overrides his feelings. He betrays the Major-General to the Pirate King despite his love for Mabel and his respect for her father: 'It breaks my heart to betray the honoured father of the girl I adore, but as your apprentice I have no alternative. It is my duty to tell you that General Stanley is no orphan!'

The Sergeant of Police articulates our feelings about Frederic. He responds to his realignment with the pirates with 'This is perplexing' – a sentiment reinforced by his constables when they add 'We cannot understand it at all'. The policemen represent a different view of the world. They also have a duty to do, but it is performed in the context of sympathy for their fellow human beings:

> When the enterprising burglar's not a-burgling,
> When the cut-throat isn't occupied in crime,
> He loves to hear the little brook a-gurgling,
> And listen to the merry village chime.
> When the coster's finished jumping on his mother,
> He loves to lie a-basking in the sun.
> Ah, take one consideration for another,
> A policeman's lot is not a happy one.
> When constabulary duty's to be done,
> A policeman's lot is not a happy one.

The Sergeant of Police was originally played by Rutland Barrington, whose rotund figure and droll manner reminded the audience of a Dickens character. The song of which this verse is a part resounds with the benevolence of the novelist. The kindheartedness of the policemen contrasts with the mechanical virtue of Frederic and reminds us that in the nineteenth century there was a point of view which held that compassion and sympathy for human beings were more important than moral judgement. As the century wore on, there was a growing awareness that virtuous conduct alone was not enough to guarantee respectability. In *The Victorian Frame of Mind*, Walter Houghton says:

> Under the influence of Victorian benevolence, however motivated, the moral judgment of a strict conscience, taking the ten commandments for its standard, lost its central authority. It was attacked because it ignored other moral qualities over and above technical virtue, noble emotions which might even thrive in characters by no means free from sin; and because it encouraged a holier-than-thou self-righteousness that was fatal to the development of compassion.[4]

Frederic is a paragon of technical virtue. From the standpoint of duty, his actions are impeccable; but from an attitude of compassion, he is clearly an unattractive hero. In the final scene of the opera, the pirates seize Major-General Stanley and prepare to kill him. Mabel appeals to Frederic for help, but all Frederic can do is weakly utter: 'Beautiful Mabel,/I would if I could, but I am not able.' In the hour of greatest need, his conscience has rendered him impotent. It is the timid police, not Frederic, who answer Mabel's call for help and fight the pirates. Frederic is not heard from again in the opera, and although productions of the opera end with him united with Mabel, one suspects that a more fitting ending would see him rejected by her and his place taken by one of the other pirates.

Frederic is not the only character in the opera whose moral pretensions are mocked. Mabel, for example, is presented initially as the archetypal Victorian young lady devoid of sexual passion. She declares she is attracted to Frederic from 'pity's name' and her waltz-song 'Poor wandering one' is a statement of her mission to rescue him from his wayward course. Her earnestness is reminiscent of the Women's Christian Temperance Union at its best. But the female chorus knows better and gives voice to our natural suspicion about her real motives: 'The question is, had he not been/A thing of beauty,/Would she be swayed by quite as keen/A sense of duty?' After Mabel completes her song, she leaves the stage with Frederic, and whatever happens offstage is enough to cause her to cast off the mask of propriety, for when she returns she sings: 'Did ever maiden wake/From dream of homely duty,/To find her daylight break/With such exceeding beauty?' In the light of her love for Frederic, duty seems 'homely' indeed.

Sullivan's music plays an important role in demolishing Mabel's pretensions. On paper, the song 'Poor wandering one' reads like a hymn: it is full of 'thees' and 'thous' and its central image is that of a lost sheep who has wandered from the flock. Sullivan sets these words not to a hymn but to the most sensuous of nineteenth-century popular musical forms, a waltz. The tonal conflict of the words and music expresses wittily the clash of propriety and passion in Mabel.

As noted earlier, Mabel's sisters are characterised as the guardians of respectability in the opera. When Mabel leaves them to flirt with Frederic, they are caught in a dilemma:

> What ought we to do,
> Gentle sisters, say?
> Propriety, we know,
> Says we ought to stay;
> While sympathy exclaims,
> 'Free them from your tether –
> Play at other games –
> Leave them here together?

They decide on a compromise: they remain on the scene but pretend to ignore Mabel and Frederic's love-making by shutting their eyes and talking about the weather. They begin chattering noisily, but their real interest is revealed in the stage action: *'During Mabel's solo the Girls continue chatter pianissimo, but listening eagerly all the time.'* Propriety serves as a convenient mask for prurience.

The girls' father, Major-General Stanley, is not immune from similar attack. Much of his appearance in the opera is taken up with remorse at having strayed from the proper course of conduct in lying to the pirates. 'Lying', says Samuel Smiles, 'is not only dishonest, but cowardly.' As a soldier, the Major-General is fully aware of this, and his remorse is compounded by his feeling that he has brought disgrace on his ancestors. At the beginning of Act II, we discover him seated in a 'draughty old ruin' where he comes 'to humble myself before the tombs of my ancestors, and to implore their pardon for having brought dishonour on the family escutcheon.' This sounds reasonable until Frederic points out that the ancestors buried in the chapel are not the Major-General's true ancestors at all, since he only recently purchased the estate. Nonetheless, the idea that he is a 'descendant by purchase' of some ancestors gives the Major-General a satisfying sense of dishonoured family tradition. Gilbert here satirises the upwardly mobile Victorian middle class which hoped it could achieve the respectability of the aristocracy by the acquisition of money, land and property. What matters to a gentleman is that he has ancestors; it does not matter if those ancestors are real or bought.

Frederic, the Major-General, Mabel and her sisters represent the world of Victorian respectability. Each of the characters has a virtue drawn from the ideals of Victorian behaviour: Frederic's obsession with duty, the Major-General's sense of honour, Mabel's zeal for good works, and the sisters' insistence on decorum. One by one, these characters are unmasked; their true natures are shown to be different from their respectable veneers. The final blow is delivered by the irony that the pirates' world is less corrupt than the civilised world. When Frederic asks the Pirate King to accompany him back to 'civilisation', the Pirate King refuses, saying 'I don't think much of our profession, but contrasted with respectability it is comparatively honest.' In the song that follows, he says it is better to live an honest life as a pirate than 'play a sanctimonious part,/With a pirate head and a pirate heart.' The world outside the pirates' lair is a 'cheating world', where 'pirates all are well-to-do'. Indeed, the pirates lead a quietly civilised life: they have a maid, Ruth, and they accept apprentices just like any other trade. Their actions are motivated by compassion: they are too tenderhearted ever to attack an orphan, and so they set free anyone who declares himself to be one. Although implicitly a rape, their capture of the female chorus is completely free of lasciviousness. After seizing the girls, the pirates declare 'You shall quickly be parsonified/Conjugally matrimonified,/By a doctor of divinity/Who resides in the vicinity.'

The pirates' behaviour is so gentlemanly that we are not at all surprised when they turn out to be 'noblemen who have gone wrong' at the end of the opera. This magical transformation appears to restore the right order to society: the Major-General instructs the pirates-cum-peers to 'resume your ranks, and legislative duties' and as he distributes his daughters – 'all of whom are beauties' – the curtain falls.

The restoration of order at the end of *The Pirates* is not as convincing as at the end of the two previous operas. This is partly because the demolition of respectable behaviour during the opera leaves no character intact. It is also because the facetious tone is maintained right up until the fall of the curtain. It is difficult to miss the sarcasm of the Major-General's reaction to the revelation that the pirates are really noble lords: 'No Englishman unmoved that statement hears,/Because, with all our faults, we love our House of Peers.' The last-minute invocation of Queen Victoria is a burlesque touch which shows the difference in tone between *Pinafore* and *Pirates*. *Pinafore* ends on a resounding serious patriotic note with the entire cast singing 'For he is an Englishman'. In *Pirates*, such sentiment is parodied in the penultimate tableau, where the Police take out their pocket handkerchiefs and weep at the mention of the Queen's name. Instead of depositing us back in normality, *The Pirates* leaves us in a zany world where the only comforting thought is the last line of the final chorus: 'Take heart! Take heart! Take heart!'

The irreverent spirit of *Pirates* continues in *Patience*. In this opera, the target of satire is the aesthetic movement in art of the 1870s and 1880s. The opera tells of the rivalry of two aesthetic poets, Reginald Bunthorne and Archibald Grosvenor, for the love of Patience, a simple dairymaid. As in *Pirates*, the chorus plays a major role in the action. The poets are adored by a chorus of 'rapturous maidens' who go about dressed in 'aesthetic draperies' and play archaic instruments such as lutes and double pipes. The maidens are sought after by a regiment of Dragoon Guards whose military manner and bright uniforms are a vivid contrast to the effeminate posturing of the poets. In the second act, the officers of the regiment abandon their uniforms in favour of aesthetic costumes to win the affection of the maidens.

The aesthetic movement grew out of the dissatisfaction of artists such as William Morris with mid-Victorian standards in art and decoration. In place of the utilitarianism and sentimentality of Victorian design, the aesthetes substituted a new philosophy of 'art for art's sake'. This philosophy recognised 'the apotheosis of beauty as the supreme experience of life, and of art as a superior reality, atoning for the deficiencies of nature and totally unlike any other kind of human activity, with laws and values unique to it. Aestheticism thus offered the mode of experience farthest removed from anything else available in an industrial world.'[5] The worship of beauty led the enlightened to ancient Greece, the Renaissance, the Middle Ages and to the Orient for inspiration: hence Lady Jane's suggestion for reform of the Dragoons' uniform in *Patience*: 'Still, there *is* a cobwebby grey velvet, with a tender bloom like cold gravy, which, made Florentine fourteenth century, trimmed with Venetian leather and Spanish altar lace, and surmounted with something Japanese – it matters not what – would at least be Early English!'

Middle-class Victorians viewed the aesthetes as silly and affected. This view was not helped by the histrionic behaviour of Oscar Wilde who strolled through London in velvet knee-breeches and pretended to swoon at the sight of a badly-decorated house. Wilde was regarded as something of a freak, and in 1882 Richard D'Oyly Carte (ever sensitive to what would amuse the public) sent him to America for a lecture tour. The aesthetes were caricatured continuously in the comic literature and drama of the 1870s and 1880s. Gilbert's farce *Tom Cobb* (1875) concerns a young surgeon who is forced unwillingly into playing the role of aesthete. He becomes involved with the Effingham family, whose credo is: 'Withdraw within yourself. Soar. Be abstract. Think long and largely. Study the incomprehensible. Revolve. So will you learn at last to detach yourself from the sordid world, and float, as we float, in thoughts of empyrean purity.' *Patience* is full of such parody of aesthetic gobbledygook: 'There is a transcendentality of delirium – an acute accentuation of supremest ecstasy – which the earthy might easily mistake for indigestion.'

In the third act of *Tom Cobb*, the title character changes his appearance to conform with the Effingham philosophy: 'He parts his hair in the centre, and allows it to grow long. He wears a very low lie-down collar in order to look Byronic.' Such changes of outer appearance are the unifying motif of *Patience*. In the first act, Bunthorne reveals that he is an 'aesthetic sham', and his 'costume chaste/Is but good taste/Misplaced!' Colonel Calverley of the Dragoons sings a spirited song extolling the attractiveness of his military uniform, but in the second act he changes to aesthetic dress in order to win back the affection of the maidens. At the end of the opera, Grosvenor and the rapturous maidens discard the aesthetic costume and appear in everyday clothes. The change in Grosvenor is particularly surprising: '*He has had his hair cut and is dressed in an ordinary suit of dittoes and a pot hat.*'

The most original aspect of *Patience* is the conception of the title character. *Patience* marks a step forward in female characterisation in the Savoy Operas, for the heroine is the first to play a major role in the action of the story. Aline, Josephine and Mabel are ornaments: each is an attractive focus for the hero's romantic ardour but has little influence on events. The plot of *Patience*, on the other hand, depends on the game Patience plays with her suitors. In Act I, she rejects Grosvenor and accepts Bunthorne; in Act II, the reverse happens. The basis for these reversals is her idea that true love must be unselfish, and to marry a man who is perfect is selfish.

The dominant characteristic of Patience's first appearances in the opera is her innocence. In the opening scene, her sudden appearance armed with milkpail and dressed in rustic costume destroys the mood of limpid despondence created by the aesthetic maidens. Her ingenuousness heightens awareness of the ludicrousness of the female chorus. When Angela says 'Patience, if you have never loved, you have never known true happiness', the milkmaid replies, 'But the truly happy always seem to have so much on their minds. The truly happy never seem quite well.' She cannot understand the maidens' passion for Bunthorne: 'In the matter of love I am untaught. I have never loved but my great-aunt.' Later, her literalness explodes the affected speech of Bunthorne. He says, 'I am pleased with thee. The bitter-hearted one, who finds all else hollow, is pleased with thee. For you are not hollow. *Are* you?', and she replies, 'No, thanks, I have dined'. These confrontations are like those in *Pygmalion and Galatea*, Gilbert's blank-verse play of 1875, in which the innocence of a statue that comes alive is used to point out the foolishness of the world.

During the opera Patience evolves into an object of satire herself. Lady Angela tells her that 'love is the one unselfish emotion in this whirlpool of grasping greed', and Patience thereupon decides that it is her duty to fall in love with someone. Although she is in love with Grosvenor, she rejects him because to marry him would deprive the world of his perfection. At the end of Act I, she chooses Bunthorne, whose unattractiveness is a guarantee against selfishness:

> PATIENCE: True love must single-hearted be –
> From every selfish fancy free –
> No idle thought of gain or joy
> A maiden's fancy should employ –
> True love must be without alloy . . .
> It follows then, a maiden who
> Devotes herself to loving you (*indicating Bunthorne*)
> Is prompted by no selfish view.

In the second act, Patience is miserable, but maintains her engagement to Bunthorne because, as she continually recites to herself, 'it is my duty'. She is able to release herself from him when he decides to reform his manner along the lines of Grosvenor. His new perfection provides a way out:

> PATIENCE: Is it quite certain that you have absolutely reformed – that you are henceforth a perfect being – utterly free from defect of any kind?
> BUNTHORNE: It is quite certain. I have sworn it.
> PATIENCE: Then I can never be yours!
> BUNTHORNE: Why not?
> PATIENCE: Love, to be pure, must be absolutely unselfish, and there is nothing unselfish in loving so perfect a being as you have now become!

Patience's actions are based on compliance with moral ideals rather than on her true feelings. In this way, she is the female equivalent of Frederic in *Pirates*. Her obsession with unselfishness represents the most extreme side of the Victorian moral code. Walter Houghton observes that Victorian children 'were brought up to hear such constant emphasis on duty and self-sacrifice, on benevolence and sympathy . . . that they were under the necessity not only of being actuated by noble motives but of not being actuated by any that were mean, selfish, or destructive.'[6] These standards of conduct were, as Houghton remarks, 'Too high for human nature.' In *Patience*, we see the consequence of the conflict between human nature and moral duty. On one level, this conflict is comic. In a scene in Act II with Grosvenor, Patience vacillates between attraction and repulsion for the poet: 'Advance one step, and as I am a good and pure woman, I scream! *(Tenderly.)* Farewell, Archibald! *(Sternly.)* Advance at your peril! Once more, adieu!' This passage is similar to Josephine's behaviour with Ralph during Act I of *Pinafore*. In these passages we are made acutely aware of the clash between the mask society forces the characters to wear and their true feeling. In Patience's case, the mask is self-imposed, and this gives a hint of borderline insanity to the character.

The difference between Frederic and Patience is the pathos introduced in the second character. In the second act of the opera, she is trapped in an engagement with a man she does not love. Alone on stage, she sings a ballad which expresses her sadness:

> Rendering good for ill,
>   Smiling at every frown,
> Yielding your own self-will,
>   Laughing your tear-drops down;
> Never a selfish whim,
> Trouble or pain to stir;
> Everything for him,
> Nothing at all for her!

The sentiment of this song must have been recognised by many Victorian women trapped in marriages of financial or social convenience. Even in marriages where love existed, the woman was expected to play a subordinate role, suppressing her interests and desires in favour of her husband's.[7] 'Everything for him/Nothing at all for her!': such exactly was the social and legal position of women in the nineteenth century.

Like *The Pirates of Penzance*, *Patience* satirises the moral code of its audience. One important difference from its predecessor is the abandonment of melodramatic devices. Apart from one sequence where Patience and Grosvenor discover they were childhood lovers, the opera is free of unexpected discoveries, long-suppressed secrets and surprise revelations. The action is carried forward by the efforts of the characters – chorus included – to woo each other through adoption or rejection of aesthetic manners. In short, *Patience* is the closest to a pure comedy of manners that Gilbert and Sullivan came, and it demonstrates their contribution to the renaissance of wit in British stage comedy at the end of the nineteenth century.

The unifying theme of *Sorcerer*, *Pinafore*, *Pirates* and *Patience* is the tension between the individual and the laws of behaviour. In *Sorcerer* and *Pinafore*, the conflict is between the characters and the laws of caste; in *Pirates* and *Patience*, the characters struggle against the rigid dictates of moral law. These four operas are chronologically framed by two operas with overtly legal themes: *Trial by Jury* and *Iolanthe*. The chief comedy of *Trial by Jury* is its overturning of the rigid laws governing deportment in a courtroom; as the characters assume their roles as Judge, Jury, Counsel and so on, they act out their secret wishes: the Judge and Jury flirt with the attractive Plaintiff and the Judge solves the case by marrying her. Similar conflicts of private desires and public roles are seen in the characters of *Iolanthe*, where both the Lord Chancellor and the Fairy Queen must suppress their amorous feelings beneath the veneer of respectable behaviour. Everywhere in the operas, the spirit of the Mikado lurks in the background, awaiting incarnation in the town of Titipu.

6
Retreat from Satire:
'The Gondoliers'

Iolanthe was the last Gilbert and Sullivan opera to be set in Victorian England. Beginning with *Princess Ida* in 1884, the partnership entered a new phase. During the original run of *Patience* (1881), the Savoy Theatre opened; it was there that eight comic operas were presented from 1882 to 1896. Prior to this period, the relationship between author and composer was harmonious, but after 1882 the collaboration was interrupted by a series of disagreements of increasing seriousness and ill-feeling. The operas of the early phase are stylistically homogenous, but those written in the later period have a variety of approach that reflects the collaborators' attempts to find a style of work that was mutually satisfying. *Ruddigore*, a witty parody of melodrama, is a return to the mode of burlesque popular in the 1860s and 1870s; *The Yeoman of the Guard* is a throwback to the form and style of the English romantic opera. In general, the operas of this

118

phase show a retreat from satire and an increasing emphasis on music, comic characterisation and spectacle.

The most obvious cause of the changes in approach in the later operas was Sullivan's dissatisfaction. The composer wanted an increased emphasis on music and a change in Gilbert's approach to plot and characterisation. This is shown by a letter he wrote to Gilbert in 1884: 'I want a chance for the music to act in its own proper sphere – to intensify the emotional element not only of the actual words but of the situation. I should like to set a story of human interest and probability, where the humorous words would come in a humorous (not serious) situation, and where, if the situation were a tender or dramatic one, the words would be of a similar character. Then there would be a feeling of reality about it which would give a fresh vitality in writing.' The increasing emphasis on music and humorous characterisation in the later operas reflects Gilbert's acquiescence to Sullivan's demands.

There were other forces at work. One of these was the public. By the time of *Iolanthe*, there were signs that audiences were becoming tired of Gilbert's assault on their values. In *Iolanthe*, the Fairy Queen sends the Arcadian shepherd Strephon into the British Parliament to reform it. In the present version of the opera, Strephon's reforms are merely jokes. For example, he suggests that seats in the House of Lords be attained by competitive examination. In the original version of the opera, Gilbert included a song in which Strephon urges that the focus of Parliament's attention be shifted from colonial exploits to social reform at home:

Fold your flapping wings,
Soaring Legislature!

Stoop to little things –
Stoop to Human Nature!
Never need to roam,
Members patriotic,
Let's begin at home –
Crime is no exotic!
Bitter is your bane –
Terrible your trials –
Dingy Drury Lane!
Soapless Seven Dials![1]

The serious message of this song was denounced by critics such as Beatty-Kingston of *The Theatre*: 'When, therefore, a first-night's audience, prepared to laugh itself sore, and in great measure consisting of Mr. Gilbert's avowed admirers, finds that gentleman exhibiting a tendency to import pathos and politics into a "book" like that of "Iolanthe", it may be excused for expressing disappointment as well as surprise – the more so because his pathos smacks of anger, a passion altogether out of place in a "fairy opera", and his politics are bitterly aggressive.' Gilbert had the flapping wings of his satire clipped, and promptly withdrew the offending song from the opera.

In the next opera, *Princess Ida*, there is an obvious dilution of satire by romance and spectacle. This is the first Gilbert and Sullivan opera not set in Victorian England; the setting is not specified in the text (a mysterious reference to 'Hungary' towards the end does more to confuse than enlighten) but the design scheme of the original production suggests the Middle Ages. This setting gives the opera a fairy-tale atmosphere reminiscent of a Planché extravaganza – an association reinforced by the large number of excruciating puns in the dialogue.

The satirical topic of the opera, higher education for women, was entirely relevant in 1884, but is contained in a piece where musical and theatrical values are dominant. The score is regarded as one of Sullivan's finest,[2] and there are three changes of scenery along with plenty of melodramatic stage action. In the midst of these distractions, the theme is lost; but this is perhaps just as well. Gilbert does not regard Princess Ida's feminism with any seriousness at all. Women are viewed as hopelessly ill-adapted for higher education: in one scene, one of the students is reprimanded because a sketch of a perambulator is found in her notebook. Ida herself is endowed with feminine propriety. When she instructs her ladies to help her injured brothers, she says, 'Bind up their wounds – but look the other way.'

The submersion of Victorian topicality in fantasy in *Princess Ida* links it to its successor, *The Mikado*. With one notable exception (*Utopia, Limited*), the operas that followed *The Mikado* show a decreased emphasis on social satire with its replacement by genial frivolity. *The Gondoliers* (1889) is typical of the later operas. Its theme – class distinction *versus* egalitarianism – hearkens back to *Pinafore*, but the topic is diluted to the level of weak tea when compared to the bracing spirits of *Pinafore*. The two chief characters, Marco and Giuseppe Palmieri, are Venetian gondoliers who are ardent republicans. One of them is the heir to the throne of the mythical country of Barataria, but which is not clear because the gondolier who raised them could not remember which was his son and which the prince. Until the exact identity of the heir is known, Don Alhambra del Bolero, the Grand Inquisitor of Spain, arranges for Marco and Giuseppe to reign jointly. The gondoliers seize the opportunity to reform the Baratarian monarchy along republican principles. In the opening scene of Act II, we see the results of their experiment: '*The Gondoliers are discovered, dressed, some as courtiers, officers of rank, etc., and others as private soldiers and servants of various degrees. All are enjoying themselves without reference to social distinctions.*' Don Alhambra is horrified by this demolition of class distinction, for he believes that 'in every Court, there are distinctions that must be observed'. He sings a song showing that egalitarianism leads to mediocrity; the chorus line is 'When every one is somebodee,/Then no-one's anybody!' Like *The Sorcerer* and *H.M.S. Pinafore*, the opera ends with an affirmation of the *status quo*. Neither Marco or Giuseppe is the king; this honour is reserved for Luiz, the servant of the Duke of Plaza-Toro. His coronation re-establishes the proper social order in Barataria:

> Then hail, O King of a Golden Land,
> And the high-born bride who claims his hand!
> The past is dead, and you gain your own,
> A royal crown and a golden throne!
> (*All kneel; Luiz crowns Casilda.*)

The gondoliers abandon their republican experiment and as they prepare to return to Venice, the curtain falls.

The political issues raised in the opera are de-emphasised in a number of ways. Unlike *Pinafore*, set squarely in England in 1878, *The Gondoliers* is set in a time and period remote from its writing. The scenes are Venice and 'Barataria'; the time, 1750. These temporal and geographic shifts soften the satire of the opera by placing it in the realm of fantasy. We are not as aware of this as a Victorian audience: to us, *Pinafore* is as much a period piece as *Gondoliers*. For the original audience, the fanciful settings and costumes of *The Gondoliers* signalled an escape from direct satirical attack.

In *Pinafore*, the theme of rank is introduced in the opening scene. In *Gondoliers*, there is a long delay before introduction of the topic of republicanism. It is not until three-quarters of the way through the first act that Marco and Giuseppe's political ideas are revealed. Even then, there is doubt as to their sincerity. Although they claim to hold kings 'in detestation', they quickly modify their attitude when Don Alhambra offers them the job of reigning in Barataria. The quartet 'Then one of us will be a Queen' displays an enthusiasm for reigning that is difficult to reconcile with republic ideas:

> Oh, tis a glorious thing, I ween,
> To be a regular Royal Queen!
> No half-and-half affair, I mean,
> But a right-down regular Royal Queen!

In this respect the heroes of *The Gondoliers* are quite different from Frederic in *Pirates*, who never relaxes his principles. Frederic is the slave of duty, and the events of the plot depend on the shifting alliances of his conscience, but Marco and Giuseppe are not the slaves of republicanism, and their political views have little influence on the development of the story. At the end of the first act, they are separated from their brides when they leave Venice to assume the throne of Barataria. This separation of lovers – which forms the basis of the plots of all the operas – occurs not because of the gondoliers' republican ideas but because of the exigencies of the melodramatic plot.

Like *Pinafore*, and *Pirates*, the form of *The Gondoliers* is based on the conventions of melodrama. Several plot devices used in *Pinafore* reappear. Marco and Giuseppe were mixed up as babies, just as Captain Corcoran and Ralph were. The last-minute revelation of the true identity of the king of Barataria by the nurse Inez is similar to Buttercup's confession at the end of *Pinafore*. Structurally, however, the opera is rather feeble. Suspense is maintained tenuously for two hours on the thin thread of awaiting a single piece of information: the true identity of the king of Barataria. In Act I, Don Alhambra tells the four lovers:

> Your separation will be very brief.
> To ascertain which is the King
>   And which the other,
> To Barataria's Court I'll bring
>   His foster-mother;
> Her former nurseling to declare
>   She'll be delighted.
> That settled, let each happy pair
>   Be reunited.

From this moment to the end of the opera, there is little dramatic action. The events that occupy our time in the second act are the arrivals in Barataria of each group of characters introduced in Venice in Act I. The first group to arrive are the contadine, who are eager to know which of the gondoliers is king. The answer to the question is postponed until Inez appears, and in the meantime the arrival of the women is celebrated with a dance. Don Alhambra is the next to arrive, and most of his scene is taken up with his reaction to the reforms that Marco and Giuseppe have instituted in the Baratarian monarchy. He reveals to the gondoliers that one of them was married in infancy, but since the audience already knows this, it is

124

hardly a great surprise. The Duke and Duchess of Plaza-Toro are the last group to arrive. Their lengthy scene is interrupted by three songs which have a tenuous relationship to the development of the plot at this point. The first, the Duchess' 'On the day when I was wedded' describes how the Duchess 'tamed' her husband; the second, the Duke and Duchess' duet, illustrates their professional functions; and the third, the Gavotte 'I am a courtier grave and serious' is the Duke's attempt to teach Marco and Giuseppe courtly manners. The overall effect is that of marking time until Inez arrives with news that everyone has been waiting to hear. Of course, these musical numbers are enjoyable in their own right. They are full of wit – such as the Duke and Duchess' statement that 'We enjoy an interment' – and they provide much opportunity for clever staging and dancing. In *The Pirates of Penzance*, the songs help to tell the story; in the second act of *The Gondoliers*, the story is an excuse for the fun of the musical numbers. In other words, *The Gondoliers* is much closer to a musical comedy than the earlier operas.

The implicit anti-monarchism of the opera is of doubtful relevance. Two years before the writing of the opera, Queen Victoria celebrated her Golden Jubilee, and the festivities indicated the popularity and stability of the English monarchy. The importance of *The Gondoliers* as a social document is that it reflects the changing view of the monarchy and the aristocracy in the late nineteenth century. As David Thomson says, 'the succession of attractive monarchs from Queen Victoria onwards created a new type of royal authority, resting not on constitutional prerogatives or political activity, but on the psychological needs of nationalism and imperialism and on the love of the masses of what Bagehot called "nice and pretty events".'[3] The new conception was a figurehead giving a focus to nationalism – a conception unchanged to the present day. The Duke and Duchess of Plaza-Toro are symbols of the new aristocracy. Their job is outlined in the duet in the second act: 'To help unhappy commoners, and add to their enjoyment,/Affords a man of noble rank congenial employment.' The duties listed in this song – giving out awards, laying foundation stones, giving speeches at 'charity dinners' – are still the conspicuous activities of royalty.

In March 1891, Queen Victoria selected *The Gondoliers* as the opera to be presented in command performance at Windsor Castle. This act signifies the harmlessness of the opera's satirical elements. After commenting on the prettiness of the setting, the wit of the dialogue, and the obesity of Rutland Barrington (cast as one of the heroes), the Queen concluded in her diary: 'Everyone was much pleased.'[4]

The relative weakness of *The Gondoliers* from a satirical viewpoint is compensated by the richness of its musical and theatrical qualities. The early operas have a simple musical structure based on the English romantic opera tradition of alternating dialogue with songs. The music is generally subservient to the comprehension of words and only achieves dominance at key points such as the finales. The score of *The Gondoliers* is more complex. Abandoning the single short opening chorus which was a feature of all the earlier operas except *Yeomen*, Gilbert and Sullivan begin the piece with a continuous musical scene occupying 52 of the score's 225 pages. Again at variance with the pattern of previous operas, the male and female choruses are present onstage together right from the start. Sullivan thus has at his disposal the full range of vocal parts. The action of this scene – the arrival of Marco and Giuseppe and their choice of brides – is set entirely to music. The graceful female chorus, 'List and learn', is followed immediately by the entrance of the gondoliers and their jolly 'For the merriest fellows are we'. The arrival of Marco and Giuseppe marks a shift into the Italian language and musical idiom, with the duet 'We're called gondolieri' set in a Neapolitan folk-song style. The game of blind man's buff that follows is a simple chant. The sequence reaches its climax in the next number, 'Thank you, gallant gondolieri', which begins with a startling musical surprise: after a few bars of introduction in waltz tempo, Gianetta begins singing in two-four time. She and the sopranos continue singing in this rhythm, while the remainder of the voices accompany with 'Tra-la' in three-four. The effect is exhilarating, and at the end the characters dance off the stage two by two.

This general coupling of principals and chorus usually takes place at the *end* of the other operas. Contrary to this pattern, *The Gondoliers* begins with mating and celebration. The festive atmosphere established in the opening scene is never seriously threatened by subsequent events.

There is a larger cast of principal characters in *Gondoliers* compared to earlier operas. The year 1889 was one of dispute and change in the Savoy Company: George Grossmith and Richard Temple left the company, and Gilbert had a disagreement with Jessie Bond over her salary. The result of this turmoil was an overhaul of the stock system of casting on which the earlier operas were based. Determined to suppress the egoism of his leading performers, Gilbert decided to write an opera with not one hero and heroine, but three pairs of lovers, each of whom is given equal weighting in the libretto. This led to an expanded score, since each character is permitted one major solo number. 'When a merry maiden marries', sung by Tessa, is balanced by 'Kind, sir, you cannot have the heart' (Gianetta), and Giuseppe's 'Rising early in the morning' is given equal time in Marco's 'Take a pair of sparkling eyes'. The emphasis on the young romantic leads in the libretto and score contributes to the opera's spirit of youthful gaiety.

In addition to greater musical complexity, there is more emphasis on visual effects than in earlier operas. Images of Mediterranean brightness are dotted through the opera: the opening scene makes reference to 'summer skies', the 'shimmering blue', and 'the emerald sea'. The scene at opening transforms these images into visual effect. The setting is the Piazzetta, Venice: in the background is the 'shimmering blue' of the lagoon; in the foreground, the chorus of contadine tying bouquets of roses. A few moments later, Marco and Giuseppe glide onto stage on a gondola, and they are assailed by the girls, who cover them with the flowers. The floral visual image is stunning and apt, for the overall mood of the opera is happiness.

Movement fills the opera from beginning to end. Instead of standing in polite rows observing the action, the chorus is always involved in stage action: tying roses, hauling a boat alongside the quay, helping in the game of blind man's buff. At the opening of the second act, the members of the male chorus are individualised into different members of the Court of Barataria, and the stage is alive with activity: *'some playing cards, others throwing dice, some reading, others playing cup and ball, "morra", etc.'* There is also a greater emphasis on dance than in previous operas. In *Pirates*, the dances are 'incidental' – that is, they consist of a few steps scattered here and there in the musical numbers and the finale. In addition to incidental dances, *Gondoliers* has two formal dances written into the score. The first is the Cachucha celebrating the arrival of the girls in Barataria. Barataria is somewhere in Spain, and the Cachucha is a Spanish dance which Sullivan renders with a sensuality that is most un-Victorian. The words of the song suggest a Bacchanalian revel: 'Wine, when it runs in abundance, enhances/The reckless delight of that wildest of dances!' With its Latin rhythm maintained by pulsating brasses the music supports a scene of abandonment to pleasure that is unequalled elsewhere in the operas. The second dance is quite different. It is the stately Gavotte danced by the Duke and Duchess of Plaza-Toro and the gondoliers as part of the duke's lesson in etiquette. The contrast of its gentle courtliness with the sensuality of the Cachucha expresses the difference between the refined aristocratic world of the Plaza-Toros and the youthful vigour of the gondoliers.

As in other operas, Gilbert times the appearance of major characters with theatrical effect. At the end of the opening scene, after the gondoliers and contadine have danced off, the stage is empty for a moment, and then:

Flourish. A gondola arrives at the Piazzetta steps, from which enter the Duke of Plaza-Toro, the Duchess, their daughter Casilda, and their attendant Luiz, who carries a drum. All are dressed in pompous but old and faded clothes.

The seediness of this group of characters is a surprise on a stage that until moments before has been filled with the vitality, colour, sound and movement of the choruses. A more exciting moment occurs in the second act when the ominous figure of Don Alhambra suddenly appears to cut short the Cachucha:

> *The dance is interrupted by the unexpected appearance of Don Alhambra, who looks on with astonishment. Marco and Giuseppe appear embarrassed. The others run off, except Drummer Boy, who is driven off by Don Alhambra.*

The Duke and Duchess of Plaza-Toro and Don Alhambra are the main comic characters of *The Gondoliers*. The Duke, a Dickensian figure, is a nobleman fallen on hard times who expects like Mr Micawber to be restored from his state of impecunity. He is continuously embarrassed and hurt by the lack of pomp and ceremony that surrounds him:

DUKE: Where are the halbadiers who were to have had the honour of meeting us here, that our visit to the Grand Inquisitor might be made in becoming state?

LUIZ: Your Grace, the halbadiers are mercenary people who stipulated for a trifle on account.

DUKE: How tiresome! . . . And the band who were to have the honour of escorting us? I see no band!

LUIZ: Your Grace, the band are sordid persons who require to be paid in advance.

To rectify his financial embarrassment, he turns himself into a Limited Company, and by the second act, his financial position has changed so that he is dressed in clothes of the 'utmost magnificence' and is accompanied by a procession of retainers. The source of this 'unaccustomed pocket money' is the sale of his name in the endorsement of products and services such as providing references or attending ceremonies. It does not seem to matter if some of these activities are less than virtuous:

> In short, if you'd kindle
> The spark of a swindle,
>   Lure simpletons into your clutches –
>   Yes; into your clutches.
> Or hoodwink a debtor,
> You cannot do better
> Than trot out a Duke or Duchess.

In the 1880s, polite London society was shocked by members of the English nobility selling their names for advertisements for Pond's Cold Cream. Such behaviour is entirely in keeping with the Duke of Plaza-Toro, whose mission is to improve his financial situation by marrying his daughter to the heir to the Baratarian throne. The Duke is the personification of greed, but the characterisation is softened by other, more appealing characteristics, such as his cowardice – 'He led his regiment from behind/He found it less exciting.'

Don Alhambra is a more sinister character. He is the pivotal figure of the story. The Duke and Duchess of Plaza-Toro come to him to learn the whereabouts of Casilda's infant husband. He identifies Marco and Giuseppe as the candidates for the throne of Barataria and arranges for them to reign. He also brings the nurse Inez to establish the true identity of the king. His knowledge and actions are shrouded in mystery: when he identifies Luiz as the son of the nurse to whom the Baratarian heir was entrusted, Luiz exclaims 'Heavens, how did he know that?' The Don says, 'My young friend, a Grand Inquisitor is always up to date.'

His courtesy and reserve are spiced with a hint of sadism and more than a suggestion of lechery. When Giuseppe discovers that Inex is waiting offstage in the torture chamber, Don Alhambra says, 'There's no hurry – she's all right. She has all the illustrated papers.' A predilection for young females is evident when he meets Casilda: 'So this is the little lady who is so unexpectedly called upon to assume the functions of Royalty! And a very nice little lady, too!' In the second act, he rhapsodises to Marco and Giuseppe: 'the daughter – the beautiful daughter! aha! Oh, you're a lucky dog, one of you!' A few lines later, his attention shifts to Tessa and Gianetta, whom he describes as 'two such extremely fascinating and utterly irresistible little ladies!'

Don Alhambra is a descendant of a long line of elderly lechers in the operas. *Trial by Jury*, *Pinafore*, *Iolanthe* and *Yeomen* all have an older, physically unattractive male character who is a rival to the hero for the attentions of the heroine. In *Trial by Jury*, the Judge's inclinations are shown in the stage directions:

> *The Judge, having taken a great fancy to First Bridesmaid, sends her a note by Usher, which she reads, kisses rapturously, and places in her bosom. Enter Plaintiff. . . . The Judge . . . directs Usher to take the note from First Bridesmaid and hand it to Plaintiff, who reads it, kisses it rapturously, and places it in her bosom.*

In *Trial*, the Judge marries the Plaintiff; but it is not so in other operas. Josephine is 'nauseated' by the attentions of Sir Joseph Porter, whom she finds 'tedious, fretful, and dictatorial'. The Lord Chancellor likewise fails to win Phyllis's attention. His introductory song paints an amusing picture of frustrated sexual urges. Day in and day out, he sits in the Court of Chancery presiding over the dispensation of 'pretty young Wards in Chancery,/All very agreeable girls – and none/Are over the age of twenty-one.' He rather fancies his sexual attractiveness: 'For I'm not so old, and not so plain,/And I'm quite prepared to marry again.' His professional position prevents him from doing so, and so he watches discontentedly as others take their pick:

> With one for him – and one for he –
> And one for you – and one for ye –
> And one for thou – and one for thee –
> But never, oh, never a one for me!

The song ends with a delightfully petulant refrain, 'Which is exasperating for/A highly susceptible Chancellor!'

The sexual attraction of an older man for a younger woman is expressed with greater vigour than the 'normal' relationship between lovers of the same age. The love between the hero and heroine is usually presented in sentimental, Valentine-card idiom. For example, Strephon and Phyllis in *Iolanthe* sing:

> None shall part us from each other,
>   One in life and death are we:
> All in all to one another –
>   I to thee and thou to me!

The origin of this difference is probably Gilbert's own attraction for young women. In his autobiography, Seymour Hicks described Gilbert as 'incapable of geniality, especially in the company of men, though being a great admirer of pretty women he took endless trouble to amuse them.'[5]

Don Alhambra's eye for pretty women occurs in an opera where a large number of characters have obvious romantic and sexual appeal. The curtain rises on a group of young women described as 'young and fair/And amiable besides'. There is (as noted above) an increased number of youthful principals compared to previous operas. The three pairs of lovers are physically attractive: indeed, Marco and Giuseppe are described as 'so peerless in their beauty/That they shame the summer skies.' The physical sensuousness reaches a climax in the Cachucha of Act II. In the original production the female chorus wore short skirts, and this provided additional titillation for the gentlemen of the audience: 'The attractions of *The Gondoliers* are numerous. To begin with, the chorus wore comparatively short skirts for the first time, and the gratifying fact is revealed to a curious world that the Savoy chorus are a very well-legged lot.' Times have changed since *The Pirates*, where Major-General Stanley's daughters demurely slip off their shoes to paddle in the sea.

The reviewer's comment quoted above reminds us that *The Gondoliers* was written in an age of male dominance. One of the unappealing aspects of the Savoy Operas is that women are regarded as commodities. This is seen in the Lord Chancellor's song quoted above, where a female cattle market is described. In *The Mikado*, Ko-Ko describes Yum-Yum as if she were a piece of furniture: 'Charming little girl, isn't she? Pretty eyes, nice hair. Taking little thing, altogether.' This attitude is satirised in Katisha: 'I have a left shoulder-blade that is a miracle of loveliness. People come miles to see it. My right elbow has a fascination that few can resist. . . . It is on view Tuesdays and Fridays, on presentation of visiting cards.' In general, the heroines have value only in terms of their physical attractiveness, monetary wealth or loyalty.

Marco's song 'Take a pair of sparkling eyes' is a catalogue – à la Petrarch – of the most desirable features of womanhood in the nineteenth century. As Marco says, the song is a 'recipe for perfect happiness', and its imagery suggests the manufacture and ownership of a man-made product rather than the appreciation of something natural. The listener is instructed to take, to furnish, to keep, to plan, to admire – as if an inanimate object is being described. The first ingredient is 'a pair of sparkling eyes' – but the suggestion of openness and directness in the word 'sparkling' is quickly modified in the next line: 'Hidden, ever and anon, in a merciful eclipse.' Direct eye contact is a sign of forwardness, an undesirable feature in a Victorian woman, who was expected to assume an attitude of coy bashfulness. The eclipse is 'merciful': this suggests that it protects us from the sudden loss of self-control that might occur if we are subjects to a full gaze. Having managed to navigate safely past the eyes, we move quickly – lest we be seen to linger too long on areas that might overstimulate – past 'a pair of rosy lips' and 'a figure trimly planned' to arrive at a sexually safe area, the hand. The hand that greets us is 'tender' and 'little' – suggesting weakness and a need for protection. Lastly, as if the speaker is describing a tablecloth in a linen shop, the hand is 'fringed with dainty fingerettes'. This bizarre image reinforces the idea of a gaudily decorated object. In the second verse this concoction of 'treasures rich and rare' furnishes a 'pretty little cot' – an action symbolising the nineteenth-century view that a woman's place was in the home. There is no hint of irony or parody in this song, which shows that Gilbert was a true Victorian in his views of women.

Two female characters in *The Gondoliers* deserve special mention because they show the change in tone in the later operas. The first is Casilda, the daughter of the Duke and Duchess of Plaza-Toro, who was wed in babyhood to the infant son of the King of Barataria. At the beginning of the opera, she is in an identical situation to Josephine in *Pinafore*, for she has fallen in love with a man below her social station: Luiz, the servant of her father. The Duke wishes her to honour her childhood marriage, and so she is placed in the same dilemma as Josephine – in short, a conflict between love and duty. This dilemma leads Josephine into a quagmire of indecision from which she emerges only in the second act. Her inner conflict focuses the audience's attention on the themes of the opera. Casilda is quite different. With scarcely any thought, she chooses the path of duty and rejects Luiz:

> LUIZ: But you will not recognise this marriage? It took place when you were too young to recognise its import.
>
> CASILDA: Nay, Luiz, respect my principles and cease to torture me with vain entreaties. Henceforth my life is another's.

When Luiz appeals to her once more, the firmness of her reply indicates that her mind is made up: 'Luiz, it must be so.' Later in the opera, she suggests that she is not completely happy with the situation, but she never experiences the lengthy internal debates of Josephine. On her arrival in Barataria, she tells her parents, 'Well, whatever happens, I shall, of course, be a dutiful wife, but I can never love my husband.' This thought does not perturb her; love is an annoyance she is willing to

136

overlook in favour of duty. The absence of inner conflict in this character suggests that Gilbert was deliberately attempting to keep the material of *The Gondoliers* as light as possible.

The other character of interest is the Duchess of Plaza-Toro. In the early operas, the principal contralto part is an unmarried middle-aged female who is often in love with the hero. The prototype of this character is the 'rich attorney's elderly, ugly daughter' in the Judge's song in *Trial by Jury*. Her appearance is immortalised in two lines: 'She may very well pass for forty-three/In the dusk, with a light behind her!' The full development of this figure is seen in Ruth in *The Pirates of Penzance*. Her age and physical appearance are the butt of the pirates' jokes, and despite the difference in their ages – Ruth is 47, Frederic 21 – she is romantically attracted to Frederic. An early scene in the opera depicts her entreaties to take her with him when he leaves the pirate band. Frederic is almost persuaded, but Major-General Stanley's daughters appear in the distance. He sees the difference between their beauty and Ruth's ugliness, and bitterly denounces her:

> FRED: You told me you were fair as gold!
> RUTH: And, master, am I not so?
> FRED: And now I see you're plain and old.
> RUTH: I am sure I am not a jot so.
> FRED: Upon my innocence you play.
> RUTH: I'm not the one to plot so.
> FRED: Your face is lined, your hair is grey.
> RUTH: It's gradually got so.

There is more than a hint of cruelty in the references to wrinkles, grey hair and plainness. The scene is rendered

137

tolerable only by Sullivan's music for the subsequent duet, where Ruth's words are set to a tender melody that supplies the pathos missing in the words. After the duet, Ruth leaves the stage and returns only – out of masochism, perhaps? – to be repudiated once more by Frederic during the Act I finale.

Much debate has raged over Gilbert's alleged lack of taste in the depiction of characters such as Ruth.[6] In his period, he was not alone in poking fun at middle-aged females with amorous intentions. For example, Penelope Ann in *Box and Cox* is a 'still blooming though somewhat middle aged widow' whom both Box and Cox have tried to evade. The sequence in *Box and Cox* where the two characters try to foist her off on each other is identical to the scene in *Pirates* where the Pirate King and Frederic argue about Ruth's fate. With mock generosity, Cox says, 'You are much more worthy of her than I am, sir. Permit me, then, to follow the generous impulse of my nature – I give her up to you.' Frederic's parallel line is 'I will not be so selfish as to take her from you. In justice to her, and in consideration to you, I will leave her behind.'

Despite the ubiquity of this figure in Victorian farce and comedy, Sullivan objected to its inclusion in his comic operas. By the time of *The Mikado*, the conception of the principal contralto role changed so that in addition to comical elements there were compassion and pathos. Katisha has the physical grotesquerie of earlier characters: she is unattractive ('my face is plain') and there are suggestions of Amazonian size: 'As for my circulation, it is the largest in the world.' The images with which she is associated include lions and tigers, tempests and torrents. Despite these unpleasant associations, Katisha is the one figure in the opera whom Gilbert and Sullivan deliberately humanise. In both acts, she is given moments when she bares her soul. In Act I, it is during the finale ('The hour of gladness') and in Act II she sings one of Gilbert's most poignant lyrics:

> Hearts do not break!
> They sting and ache
> For old love's sake,
> But do not die,
> Though with each breath
> They long for death
> As witnesseth
> The living I!
> Oh, living I!
> Come, tell me why,
> When hope is gone,
> Dost thou stay on?
> Why linger here,
> Where all is drear?
> Oh, living I!
> Come, tell me why,
> When hope is gone,
> Dost thou stay on?
> May not a cheated maiden die?

Katisha is one of the hardest roles in the Gilbert and Sullivan canon to play. For most of the opera a grotesque figure, rejected and mocked by others, in these songs she expresses her true feelings. There is no way for an actress to make these moments comical: Sullivan's music will simply not allow it. Through his music, we come to believe in Katisha's hopeless love for Nanki-Poo more than we believe in the feelings between any other characters.

There is no trace of either Ruth or Katisha in the

Duchess of Plaza-Toro. Compared with the earlier contralto roles, the Duchess is an insignificant and unoriginal character. She is a familiar type: the domineering middle-aged wife whose main function is to supply witty ripostes to her husband's remarks. When the Duke tells the gondoliers that Casilda will 'make you happier than her mother has made me', the Duchess interjects a stern 'Sir!', and he quickly adds 'If possible'. This kind of badinage between husband and wife is a well-worn device of stage comedy. The unoriginality of the character influenced Sullivan, who supplied a repetitiously oom-pah-oom-pah musical accompaniment to her one solo number.

The Gondoliers substitutes music, dance, spectacle, festivity and romance for the burlesque and social satire of the earlier operas. Two reasons for this change have been mentioned already: Sullivan's insistence on greater 'human interest' in the libretti, and criticism of the political comments in *Iolanthe*. A third factor which influenced the style of the operas was the appearance of competitors. When Gilbert and Sullivan began their partnership, they were practically alone in writing musical works of quality and originality in English. By the 1880s, other writers of talent emerged and produced musical plays that competed with the fare at the Savoy. The new musical plays of the 1880s did not have the same satiric emphasis as the Savoy Operas; they were entertainments that stressed clever musical numbers, pretty scenery, dancing and spectacle. In 1886, the success of *Dorothy*, a comic opera by Alfred Cellier, took both Sullivan and D'Oyly Carte by surprise: the piece achieved a run of 931 performances, greater than any Savoy Opera. Gilbert's reaction was characteristic. Declaring that 'we are as much an institution as Westminster Abbey', he claimed that he would never change the format of the Savoy Operas to fit in with a changing taste in musical entertainment. Nonetheless, the frivolity of *The Gondoliers* shows that Gilbert was not immune to the influence of the box office.

7
Gilbert and Sullivan in Performance

Discussion of Gilbert and Sullivan is incomplete without consideration of the original performance conditions of the opera, for the Savoy Operas were not written for general publication but for performance by a particular company at a specific theatre. The size and format of the Savoy Theatre, together with the dramatic and vocal resources of its company, influenced the style of the scores and libretti and thus indirectly still influence the performance style best suited to the operas.

The first point of interest is the physical environment in which the operas were originally performed. The original Savoy (opened in October 1881) was completely reconstructed in 1929, but its scale can be appreciated from contemporary illustrations and comments. Unfortunately, many of these sources give a false impression of its size; for example, a much-reproduced drawing of the interior printed in the *Graphic* of December 1881 shows an audience watching a scene from *Patience*, and the small size of the figures on stage exaggerates the theatre's size. A much more truthful picture is provided by a 1907 photograph reprinted in Baily[1] which shows Gilbert reading the libretto of *Fallen Fairies* to the cast seated in the stalls. By modern standards, the theatre looks quite cramped: a 'Way out' sign at the back of the auditorium is clearly visible.

A description in *The Builder's News* of 23 September 1881 corroborates the intimacy of the theatre. The stage opening was 30 feet wide by 32 feet high; on either side of the stage there were three levels of private boxes. The auditorium was arranged in tiers of horseshoe-shaped balconies. On the main floor, there were nine rows of stall seats and six rows of pit seats, making for a total of only fifteen rows of seats from the orchestra pit to the back of the auditorium. Above the main floor, there was a dress circle of six rows; above this, an upper circle of five rows. The final levels were an amphitheatre and gallery which had a total of eight rows. This vertical arrangement of seating permitted maximum capacity without loss of rapport between performer and audience. (The tiers also symbolised the social stratification of Victorian society comically mirrored on stage.)

Like other nineteenth-century English playhouses, the Savoy was a proscenium theatre where the edges of the stage opening served as a picture frame for an illusion of reality. The world within the picture frame was dominated by Gilbert. Publicly, he said the success of the operas was due to 'the fact that Arthur Sullivan and I were in a commanding position. We controlled the stage altogether, and were able to do as we wished, so far as the limitations of our actors would allow of it.'[2] The truth was that Gilbert held the commanding position. His intellect and imagination dominated every phase of production from drafting the plot to selecting the fabrics used in the costumes. His artistic aim was to present within the Savoy's picture frame a pleasing and accurate representation of reality. At home, he had a miniature stage where he carefully worked out the staging of each opera before rehearsal began. In the sets and costumes, he insisted on meticulous accuracy and detail. Gifted as an amateur artist and photographer, he designed costumes for two operas (*Patience* and *Iolanthe*). For other operas, he engaged professional designers for settings and costumes, but their role was largely nominal since Gilbert scrutinised each sketch fastidiously. His major concern was for authenticity and realism. The costumes for *The Mikado*, for example, were copies of Japanese originals. For some characters, copies were not good enough: Katisha's costume was an original two-hundred-year-old dress. The obsession with accuracy extended to fabric: the dresses of the female chorus were made from pure Japanese silk imported by Liberty's. In other operas, Gilbert's greatest concern was with authenticity of military uniforms: the chorus of Bucks and Blades in *Ruddigore* was dressed in the exact uniforms worn by cavalry and infantry officers during the Napoleonic Wars.

Gilbert's supervision of staging and design at the Savoy was a reflection of trends in European theatre in the late nineteenth century. The original productions of the operas from 1875 to 1896 occurred during a period of rapid change in theatrical practice. The major development was the recognition of the need for unity in theatrical production. Early nineteenth-century theatrical production was largely a disjointed affair. Rehearsals were non-existent or inadequate; staging was haphazard; and settings and costumes were drawn from collections of stock pieces. The unifying force of the stage director did not exist. The earliest reformers were actor-managers such as William Charles Macready (1793–1873) and Charles Kean (1811–68), whose revivals of Shakespeare were carefully planned and executed. In his memoirs, Macready wrote of the difficulty of getting actors to accept the idea of rehearsal. His reply to the actor who said, 'Sir, I can never act at rehearsal, but I will do it at night' was 'Sir, if you cannot do it in the morning, you cannot do it at night.'

Macready and Kean were followed by other actor-managers who attempted to stamp individual style on presentations. The most notable contemporary of Gilbert and Sullivan was Henry Irving (1838–1905), who managed the Lyceum Theatre from 1878 to 1898. Irving's repertoire was a strange mixture of melodramas such as *The Bells* and classical revivals. All of his productions were dominated by his personality; as Frances Donaldson observes, 'He saw the picture as a whole and in the middle of the picture he saw himself.'[3]

The drive for unity in production in the English theatre was stimulated by Continental ideas. In Bayreuth, Richard Wagner (1813–83) achieved a synthesis of music, spectacle and drama in his music-dramas. His productions were first seen in London in 1882. The way was prepared a year earlier by the visit to England of the Meiningen Players, the court troupe of Georg II, Duke of Saxe-Meiningen. Unlike other aristocrats who sustained court theatres, Georg took a personal interest in its endeavours. He designed and directed all the company's productions, and as a result of his efforts he has been called the first modern stage director. His productions were carefully thought out and scrupulously rehearsed; every detail of stage action was planned in terms of its contribution to

145

the overall effect. When the company gave a season at Drury Lane in 1881, it was especially praised for its realistic portrayal of crowd scenes.

A further stimulus came from the desire of dramatists to have more say in the production of their plays. In the early nineteenth century, playwrights sold their plays to managers who then produced them in whatever way they liked. By the 1860s, there were signs of change. The first major dramatist-director of the English theatre was Tom Robertson (1829–71) who worked for the Bancrofts at the Prince of Wales' Theatre in the 1860s. Robertson supervised the presentation of all six of his comedies from *Society* (1865) to *The M.P.* (1870). His major contribution was the insistence on detail in setting and performance which is reflected in the lengthy stage directions in his plays. (In fact, Robertson's stage directions make him the first readable playwright of the nineteenth century.) In 1904, Gilbert summarised Robertson's contributions:

Why, he invented stage management. It was an unknown art before his time. Formerly, in a conversation scene for instance, you simply brought down two or three chairs from the flat and placed them in a row in the middle of the stage, and people sat down and talked, and when the conversation was ended the chairs were replaced. Robertson shows how to give life and variety and nature to the scene, by breaking it up with all sorts of little incidents and delicate by-play. I have been at many of his rehearsals and learnt a great deal from them.[4]

Robertson lured Gilbert into the theatre in 1866 by arranging for him to write a Christmas piece for the St

James's Theatre. During his early dramatic career, Gilbert emulated Robertson's technique as a director, but his desire to control the productions of his plays brought him into conflict with actors and actresses who were not used to direction. Gilbert's brusque manner did not help: according to Madge Kendal, he had a nasty habit of yelling from the darkened auditorium, 'What on earth do you think you are doing?'

Henry Lytton, who performed in the operas from 1887 to 1934, recalled the demands that Gilbert placed on his performers at the Savoy:

> When everything else was perfect, I have known Gilbert to spend many long hours making his company practise facial expressions, tiny movements of the hands and feet, impressing upon them the effects these small things had upon the audience and upon the general success of the piece. A rehearsal with Gilbert was a fatiguing business, but it was invariably well worth all the painstaking which he insisted should be put into the play before the curtain went up on the first night.[5]

Decima Moore, the creator of Casilda in *The Gondoliers*, left a more detailed account of Gilbert's method:

> Exact diction; every word to be heard at the back of the dress circle; the rhythm of the lines to be scrupulously followed. He would read a line of dialogue out, clapping his hands between the words to emphasise their rhythm, thus:
> 'I've no patience (*clap*) with the presumption (*clap*) of persons in his plebian (*clap*) position (*clap*).'
> 'Now, Miss Moore', he would say, 'again, please!' . . . and his hands would go clap . . . clap . . . clap.

Such autocratic methods seem strange in the twentieth century, when collaboration between actor and director is normal. In the 1880s, when the concept of direction was still new, this method gave the operas refreshing clarity and consistency of style.

Gilbert's insistence on realism in design also reflects the trends of his period. The tradition of archaeological realism in British theatre began in 1821 when Planché designed historically accurate costumes for Charles Kemble's production of *King John* at Covent Garden. In the 1850s Charles Kean gave the audience pamphlets listing the scholarly authorities consulted to give authenticity to his productions. During the rest of the century, technological innovations such as the introduction of electric light meant that theatre could present an increasingly more truthful illusion of reality. In the quest for truth, the stage was littered with an ever increasing clutter of furniture, decoration and properties. The climax was reached when Herbert Beerbohm Tree (1853–1917) used live rabbits in the forest scenes of *A Midsummer Night's Dream* (1900).

Gilbert's concern with realism extended beyond setting and design to acting. He promoted an acting style very different from the prevailing style of the Victorian comic stage exemplified by the cast of *Thespis*. Gilbert had no control of casting in the production of this opera, and the leading parts were taken by popular comedians who – as was the custom of the day – simply regarded the script as an excuse for the addition of their own pranks and jokes. Mercury was played by Nellie Farren, a comic actress who specialised in 'travesty' (i.e. transvestite) roles, and Thespis by J. L. Toole, a comedian whose brand of 'low' comedy was the exact opposite of Mathews' and Grossmith's style. Stupidas and Preposteros were portrayed by two pantomime clowns, the Payne brothers. The type of comic acting represented by these performers was satirised by Gilbert in an essay entitled 'Actors, Authors and Audiences' in which an unsuccessful dramatist is tried by a jury of the audience. The play's comedian is called to provide evidence in defence of the author:

> I did my best with the part. I bought a remarkably clever mechanical wig – (*laughter*) – for it – (*laughter*) – but it was useless. (*Roars of laughter*). In my zeal in behalf of the Prisoner I introduced much practical 'business' into the part that was not set down for me. (*Laughter*.) I did not charge extra for introducing practical business; I introduced it solely in the Prisoner's interest. No doubt the Prisoner remonstrated, but I know what an audience likes much better than he does. (*Laughter*.) The part was soundly hissed – even the introduced scene with the guinea-pig and the hair-oil. (*Roars of laughter*.)[6]

At the Savoy, Gilbert determined to replace the broadness of Victorian comic acting with discipline and restraint. He demanded strict adherence to the written text. In 1890, he sent a letter to Richard D'Oyly Carte complaining of Barrington's 'extraneous embellishments' of his text; he asked the stage manager to provide a daily report of all divergencies so the offender could be reprimanded. In addition to textual accuracy, Gilbert promoted a style of performance that was very different from the practices of Farren, Toole and the Paynes. Jessie Bond summarised his approach: 'He would have no horse-play, no practical joking, no make-up of the crude, red-nosed order or ridiculous travesties of dress and manner. All must be natural, well-behaved and pleasant, and the actors were trained to get their effects by doing and saying absurd things in a matter-of-fact way, without obvious burlesque of the characters they were representing.'[7]

Gilbert inherited this approach from Planché, whose Olympic Theatre burlesques of the 1830s and 1840s were played in a similar style. Ernest Watson says, 'It was Planché's belief that the highest effect in these burlesques could be achieved by having the acting perfectly natural and familiar, so that the contrast between the absurdity of the thing said and the propriety of the everyday behaviour of the speakers should greatly heighten the comic effect. Thus a new realistic technique was introduced into burlesque.'[8] His views found sympathy with Charles Mathews, who starred with Madame Vestris in Planché's plays. Mathews said that his acting aimed at 'holding the mirror up to nature without regard to the conventionalities of the theatre'.[9]

Mathews excelled in his own pieces such as *Patter Versus Clatter* where he impersonated multiple characters and delivered clever patter-songs with amazing rapidity:

When a man travels he mustn't look queer
If he gets a few rubs that he doesn't here,
And if from Calais to Paris he stray
I'll tell him the things that he'll meet on his way.
> Dover heights
> Men like mites
> Skiffery-cliffery-Shakespeare.
> Can't touch prog
> Sick as a dog
> Sackenem-rackenem makes pier.
> Calais clerks

Searchery-lurchery-fee-fee.
On the pavé
Cabriolet
Crackery-brackery-oui-oui.
Abbeville
Off went a wheel
Habbery-dabbery-tub-tub . . .

Despite the efforts of Planché and Mathews, Victorian stage comedy was dominated by the mechanical wig and the guinea-pig up to the time of Gilbert, who selected as his leading comedians George Grossmith (1847–1912) and Rutland Barrington (1853–1922) whose backgrounds were not in burlesque but in Mathews' style of light musical entertainment. George Grossmith was a 'light' comedian who created the roles of John Wellington Wells, Sir Joseph Porter, Major-General Stanley, Bunthorne, the Lord Chancellor, Ko-Ko, Robin Oakapple and Jack Point. Prior to his association with Gilbert and Sullivan he worked as a touring entertainer, performing sketches consisting of songs, jokes and impersonations to self-accompaniment on the piano. An example of Grossmith's comedy is *The Middle-Puddle Porter*:

There was a railway porter on the North South Eastern
   Line,
Whose intellect was limited, whose age was forty-nine.
His post was situated at the Muddle-Puddle Junction;
The stations' names he called out indistinctly – but with
   unction.
And all this porter had to do thro' morning, noon, and
   night
Was to waggle to and fro a wretched bell with all his
   might;

And shout this sentence in a manner which you all
   must know –
'Change here for London, Chatham, Peckham,
   Brighton, Margate Bow.'[10]

The similarity of the characters written for Grossmith at the
Savoy results from Gilbert and Sullivan's understanding of
the type of material in which he excelled. Each of the
Grossmith roles has a patter-song with a profusion of
syllables and nonsense rhymes similar to the songs of
Mathews and Grossmith. For example, here is John
Wellington Wells:

> For he can prophesy
> With a wink of his eye,
> Peep with security
> Into futurity,
> Sum up your history,
> Clear up a mystery,
> Humour proclivity
> For a nativity – for a nativity;
> He has answers oracular,
> Bogies spectacular,
> Mirrors so magical,
> Facts astronomical,
> Solemn or comical,
> And, if you want it, he
> Makes a reduction on taking a quantity!

Grossmith's gift for impersonation was exploited in songs
such as Ko-Ko's 'I've got a little list':

> And apologetic statesmen of a compromising kind,
> Such as – What d'ye call him – Thing'em-bob, and like-
>   wise – Never-mind,

152

And 'St – 'st – 'st – and What's-his-name, and also
   you-know-who –
The task of filling up the blanks I'd rather leave to
   you.
But it really doesn't matter whom you put upon the list,
For they'd none of 'em be missed – they'd none of
   'em be missed!

The important feature of Mathews', Grossmith's and
Gilbert's comic songs is the economic use of one or two
words to create a flash picture of an individual or event.
It is the performer's job to flesh out the picture through a
deft, well-timed gesture, facial expression, or change in
voice. The comedy of these songs also depends on their
rich word-play which includes rhymes, puns, alliterations
and nonsense words. These verbal tricks are appreciated
only through absolute clarity of articulation on the
performer's part.

Like Grossmith, Barrington had achieved a reputation
in small-scale musical entertainment. Before joining
Gilbert and Sullivan, he toured with Mrs Howard Paul's
Drawing Room Entertainment, a company presenting
sketches and plays similar to Grossmith's and the Reeds'.
Barrington created the roles of Dr Daly, Captain
Corcoran, the Sergeant of Police, Grosvenor,
Mountararat, King Hildebrand, Pooh-Bah, Sir Despard,
Giuseppe, King Paramount and Ludwig. While Grossmith
was diminutive and cocky, Barrington was tall, inclined
to be stout, and ironic; together, they made a perfect
comedy team. Gilbert and Sullivan wrote many witty
scenes for them; a good example is the interview between
Pooh-Bah and Ko-Ko in Act I of *The Mikado* where
Pooh-Bah resists Ko-Ko's request for his marriage
expenses. It is easy to imagine Grossmith's spry Ko-Ko

scampering after Barrington's ponderous, condescending Pooh-Bah.

The selection of Grossmith and Barrington as leading comedians was a deliberate attempt by Gilbert and Sullivan to bring the restrained style of Victorian parlour entertainment to the comic opera stage. The most interesting aspect of Gilbert's approach to comic acting is the naturalism indicated by Jessie Bond. Unfortunately, Gilbert never wrote a treatise on comic acting, but the essence of his approach is in the introductory note to *Engaged*:

> It is absolutely essential to the success of this piece that it should be played with the most perfect earnestness and gravity throughout. There should be no exaggeration in costume, make-up, or demeanour; and the characters, one and all, should appear to believe throughout in the perfect sincerity of their words and actions. Directly the characters show that they are conscious of the absurdity of their utterances the piece begins to drag.

Gilbert's desire for truthfulness in comic acting was linked to his obsession with realism in setting and costume. This is shown by his note to *The Wedding March* (1873):

> The dresses of the Wedding Party should be quaint, countrified, and rather old-fashioned in character, but not too much exaggerated. Indeed the success of the piece depends principally on the absence of exaggeration in dress and 'make-up'. The characters should rely for the fun of their parts on the most improbable things being done in the most earnest manner by persons of every-day life.

Gilbert's aim was to present within the proscenium arch of the Savoy an illusion of reality sustained by the accuracy of the sets and costumes and the naturalism of the acting. Realism fed the audience's appetite for pleasurable illusion; more significantly, it served Gilbert's comedy and satire. By paying attention to details such as the proper operation of the policemen's lamps in *Pirates* or the rigging of the ship in *Pinafore*, Gilbert created a stage world that seemed as concrete as reality. With its teapots and truncheons, the stage world was not superficially any different from the everyday world of its audience. But the mirror was curved, not flat; it distorted the normal world so that familiar characters and events were seen in a totally new way. *Trial by Jury* is a good example. The description of the costumes in an early libretto stressed the need for realism: 'Modern dresses, without any extravagance or caricature. The defendant is dressed in bridal dress. The plaintiff as a bride. The bridesmaids as bridesmaids. The Judge, Counsel and Usher, etc., should be as like their prototypes at Westminster as possible.' The opera begins in reality, but its action takes the audience further and further into a fantastic world where the normal rules of legal proceedings are upset. The court usher broadcasts his biases to the jury; the plaintiff's companions plead for the defendant; and at the end the judge marries the plaintiff. In the original productions, the culmination of this insanity was a magical transformation of the scene:

At the last 'And a good Judge too' the gong is struck for the trick change to fairyland. The canopy revolves. The fan pieces behind Judge fall. Two revolving pieces on either side of Judge come round. The rise comes up and covers bench front. The Judge and associate's desks

*open. The Chamber flats are taken away and wings
pushed on. Cloth in front of benches and Jury box are
let down and masking for same pushed on. . . . Red
fire.*[11]

The real world is here transcended and replaced by a
dream world which is similar to the nightmare vision of a
courtroom expressed by the hero of Gilbert's last play,
The Hooligan (1911).

The basic comic technique of the Savoy Operas is a
journey from reality into fantasy; more accurately, the
logical everyday world exists simultaneously with an
illogical fantasy world which intrudes into reality. A
character in a Gilbert and Sullivan opera has feet in two
universes: one real, concrete and absolute, the other
illogical, insane and fantastic. Thus, for example, at the
end of *Pinafore* the characters are not perturbed by the
sudden transformation of Ralph into the Captain and *vice
versa*. Sir Joseph simply remarks 'This is a very singular
occurrence', and then it is back to business as the various
marital dispersions of the characters are arranged. At the
end of *The Mikado*, the Mikado declares 'Nothing could
possibly be more satisfactory!' despite the obvious illogic
of Ko-Ko's explanation of Nanki-Poo's death.

The major trend in Gilbert and Sullivan production
over the past century has been away from verisimilitude
in setting and acting. For fifty years after Gilbert's death
in 1911, the D'Oyly Carte Opera Company retained the
exclusive right to professional performance of Gilbert
and Sullivan in the British Commonwealth. By 1930, all
of the operas were redesigned with the overriding
principle of abandonment of pictorial realism in favour
of greater stylisation. Charles Ricketts' designs for *The
Mikado* of 1926 were symbolic of the new trend. He

discarded the embroidered-upholstery appearance of earlier costumes and substituted lighter costumes which gave the characters the whimsical look of *origami* figures. Ko-Ko (originally dressed in a heavy gown embroidered with peacocks) now wore a costume emblazoned with stylised axe-heads and a hat with an uncanny resemblance to an executioner's block. In setting, a turning point was Peter Goffin's 1939 design for *The Yeomen of the Guard*. Previously, this opera was played against a backdrop with a realistic painting of Tower Green. Goffin replaced this with a simple set consisting of ramps, steps and walls without ornate detail. The new setting focused attention on the characters and its starkness supported the tone of the music and drama.

The disappearance of pictorial realism in design of the operas is inevitable: it reflects the general trend away from realism in twentieth-century theatre. Unfortunately, a shift into fantasy in design destroys the atmosphere of truth that was so important a part of the original productions. While the loss of realism in design may be forgiven, the departure of earnestness from the acting of the operas is a graver sin. In 1975, the National Theatre staged a revival of Gilbert's *Engaged*, and Peter Hall's criticism of the production can be levelled at many modern productions of the operas: 'everyone was playing the play as if they themselves found it funny, rather than bravely and truly'.[12] The necessity for adhering to Gilbert's approach in acting the operas can be shown by two examples. In *Ruddigore*, there is the following exchange between Rose Maybud and Dame Hannah:

HANNAH: Wither away, dear Rose? On some errand of charity, as is thy wont?

ROSE: A few gifts, dear aunt, for deserving villagers.

Lo, here is some peppermint rock for old Gaffer Gadderby, a set of false teeth for pretty little Ruth Rowbottom, and a pound of snuff for the poor orphan girl on the hill.

Rose Maybud is a parody of the virtuous heroines of melodrama; an actress's awareness of this is apt to lead to a burlesque performance with all sorts of cute gestures and winsome facial expressions. But the speech is much more effective if spoken sincerely, as if the character really believes the kindness of her errands. A sincere reading of the lines unearths their true comedy, which is the discrepancy between Rose's earnestness and the inappropriateness of her gifts. A burlesque style also has the disadvantage of distracting attention from the comic richness of the verbal images presented.

Another example in the interview between Ralph and Josephine in the first act of *Pinafore*:

JOSEPHINE: Ralph Rackstraw! (*Overcome by emotion*)

RALPH: Aye, lady – no other than poor Ralph Rackstraw!

JOSEPHINE: (*aside*) How my heart beats! (*Aloud*) And why poor, Ralph?

RALPH: I am poor in the essence of happiness, lady – rich only in never-ending unrest. In me there meet a combination of antithetical elements which are at eternal war with one another. Driven hither by objective influences – thither by subjective emotions – wafted one moment into blazing day, by mocking hope – plunged the next into the Cimmerian darkness of tangible despair, I am but a living ganglion of irreconcilable antagonisms. I hope I make myself clear, lady?

The problem with the portrayal of Ralph is similar to that with Rose Maybud. He is a parody of the sailor-hero of melodrama, but to play his speech as burlesque weakens the delicious joke at the end which depends on Ralph's belief that he really *is* making sense. With Josephine, the acting problem is her rapid vacillation from speech to aside. The usual tendency is to play the asides as melodramatic confidences to the audience. In fact, they are the expression of her true feelings; if any aspect of the performance needs exaggeration, it is her speeches to Ralph, which we know are insincere.

Many characters in the operas are similar to Josephine in the discrepancy between truthful inner feeling and false social masks. With Josephine and Patience, this conflict is expressed through the use of asides. In other characters, it is shown by a complete change of mannerism – as when Bunthorne suddenly casts off his affected posture to reveal he is an 'aesthetic sham'. Sometimes, the conflict is expressed only in stage action, as in the scene in *Pirates* where Mabel's sisters pretend to chat about the weather but listen eagerly to the lovers. An alternative level of meaning may be expressed only in music: In Mabel's waltz-song, the music has a seductiveness absent from the words. In dialogue, hidden feelings may be suggested through a subtle shift in tone of voice: for example, when Pooh-Bah suddenly reveals his urging for a 'very considerable bribe'.

The Gilbert and Sullivan operas are rich in irony and subtlety. To make the operas work in performance requires clarity of diction, sincerity of attitude, and meticulous attention to details of phrasing, facial expression and gesture. The operas were never intended to be performed as operas, using the broadness and indelicacy of stroke favoured by opera directors. They

were written for a small theatre where fine detail of
gesture and facial expression could be understood, and
for an acting company whose leading members were not
opera singers but entertainers used to an intimate style.
To present the operas in the Grand Style is to impoverish
them of their richest quality, the delight in words and
word play. The Lord Chancellor's Nightmare Song in
Iolanthe illustrates the operas' verbal brilliance:

> When you're lying awake with a dismal headache, and
> repose is taboo'd by anxiety,
> I conceive you may use any language you choose to
> indulge in, without impropriety,
> For your brain is on fire – the bedclothes conspire of
> usual slumber to plunder you:
> First your counterpane goes, and uncovers your toes,
> and your sheet slips demurely from under you;
> Then the blanketing tickles – you feel like mixed
> pickles – so terribly sharp is the pricking;
> And you're hot, and you're cross, and you tumble and
> toss till there's nothin twixt you and the ticking . . .

This song is a feast of rhyme: not only does each line
rhyme with its neighbour, but each has internal rhymes
which are both anticipated ('awake' and 'headache') and
unexpected ('slumber to plunder you'). The really
amazing feature, though, is that amidst all the artifice,
the poem makes sense; there is not one gratuitously
placed word. A comparison of Gilbert's lyrics with those
of, say, Mathews, demonstrates Gilbert's felicity in
rendering ideas into clever but comprehensible poetry.

One further example is irresistible. It is the petulant
chorus sung by the Dragoons in *Patience* when they are
rejected by the maidens:

Now is not this ridiculous – and is not this preposterous?
A thorough-paced absurdity – explain it if you can.
Instead of rushing eagerly to cherish us and foster us,
    They all prefer this melancholy literary man.
        Instead of slyly peering at us,
        Casting looks endearing at us,
Blushing at us, flushing at us – flirting with a fan;
They're actually sneering at us, fleering at us, jeering
    at us!
        Pretty sort of treatment for a military man!
They're actually sneering at us, fleering at us, jeering
    at us!
        Pretty sort of treatment for a military man!

The percussive consonants and repetitive rhymes suggest perfectly the wounded pride of a military man. As other writers have observed, it is impossible to read a passage such as this without hearing Sullivan's music. Sullivan's gift of finding the exact musical interpretation of Gilbert's words is described by Arthur Quiller-Couch:

> For the contribution which Sullivan brought was not only his genius for melody, not a wit that jumped with Gilbert's, not a separate and musical wit which revelled in parody. Priceless as these gifts undoubtedly were, above them all (I think) we must reckon the quite marvellous sense of *words* in all his musical settings. You may examine number after number of his, and the more closely you examine the more will you be convinced that no composer ever lived with an exacter appreciation of words, their meaning, their due emphasis, their right articulation.[13]

The emphasis on The Word in the Savoy Opera runs counter to the trend of modern musical theatre to dance and spectacle, but it makes the operas eminently suitable for the most intimate of modern media, television. The television camera can both give the operas their necessary air of verisimilitude and exploit the nuances of characterisation, dialogue and songs. It is to be hoped that television producers will be stimulated by the operas' richness in the future.

8
Finale: Assessment

Utopia, *Limited* (1893) is an anomaly among the late Gilbert and Sullivan operas. Its lengthy score, elaborate settings and costumes, and large cast of characters link it to its predecessor, *The Gondoliers*; its content returns to the satire of Victorian institutions of earlier operas. The plot is simple: King Paramount, ruler of a South Pacific island, decides to reform his kingdom on the principles of English civilisation. He imports an English governess, Lady Sophy, to train his daughters in English deportment, and his daughter Zara fetches from England 'six Representatives of the principal causes that have tended to make England the powerful, happy, and blameless country which the consensus of European civilisation has declared it to be'. The six 'Flowers of Progress' are Lord Dramaleigh (a British Lord Chamberlain), Captain Fitzbattleaxe (of the army), Captain Sir Edward Corcoran, K.C.B. (of the Royal Navy; the same character as in *Pinafore*), Mr Goldbury (a Company Promoter), Sir Bailey Barre, Q.C., M.P. (a lawyer), and Mr Blushington (a County Councillor). Initially, the Utopians are happy with the reforms introduced by these figures, but towards the end of the opera it becomes clear that the improvements wrought by the introduction of English civilisation have a negative side:

> These boons have brought Utopia to a standstill!
> Our pride and boast – the Army and the Navy –
> Have both been reconstructed and remodelled
> Upon so irresistible a basis
> That all the neighbouring nations have disarmed –
> And War's impossible! Your County Councillor
> Has passed such drastic Sanitary laws
> That all the doctors dwindle, starve, and die!
> The laws, remodelled by Sir Bailey Barre,
> Have quite extinguished crime and litigation:
> The lawyers starve, and all the jails are let
> As model lodgings for the working-classes!

Just as rebellion seems imminent, Princess Zara steps forward with a proposal that saves the day:

> Government by Party! Introduce that great and glorious element – at once the bulwark and foundation of England's greatness – and all will be well! No political measures will endure, because one party will assuredly undo all that the other Party has done; and while grouse is to be shot and foxes worried to death, the legislative action of the country will be at a standstill. Then there will be sickness in plenty, endless lawsuits, crowded jails, interminable confusion in the Army and Navy, and, in short, general and unexampled prosperity!

Amid this sordid picture of the real England, the curtain falls.

Finale: Assessment

The opera is a full-length development of a theme introduced in the deleted 'Fold your flapping wings' song from *Iolanthe*: the questionable morality of colonial exploits in light of the internal social problems of Britain in the late nineteenth century. *Utopia* was written at a time when English civilisation had infiltrated every continent on earth. As James Morris points out in his study of the British Empire, imperialism was based on the notion that the British people were the moral superiors of other races:

> If so much could be achieved by agitation at home, what might not be done if the moral authority of England were distributed across the earth – to tackle the evils of slavery, ignorance, and paganism at source, to teach the simpler peoples the benefits of Steam, Free Trade, and Revealed Religion, and to establish not a world empire in the bad Napoleonic sense, but a Moral Empire of loftier intent?[1]

The satire of *Utopia Limited* is based on the irony that none of the improvements that occur in Utopia after its Anglicisation have occurred in England. This disparity is emphasised in a song sung by King Paramount where he enumerates the successes of English reform. The Flowers of Progress interject with wry comments about the state of affairs in their homeland:

> Society has quite forsaken all her wicked courses,
> Which empties our police courts, and abolishes divorces.
> *Chorus*: Divorce is nearly obsolete in England.
> Our city we have beautified – we've done it willy-nilly –
> And all that isn't Belgrave Square is Strand and Piccadilly.

Chorus: We haven't any slummeries in England!
We have solved the labour question with discrimination
polished,
So poverty is obsolete and hunger is abolished.
Chorus: We are going to abolish it in England!

The blend of politics and fantasy in *Utopia Limited*
anticipates the later plays of George Bernard Shaw
(1856–1950). Shaw reviewed the original production of
Utopia for the *Saturday Review*. The topic of Gilbert and
Sullivan opera was one of the very few on which Shaw
never wrote a lengthy essay, but comments scattered
through his reviews and letters give a general impression
of his attitude towards the operas. He had high regard
for Sullivan, and thought that the excellence of his scores
derived from

> a consummate *savoir faire* which was partly, no doubt,
> a personal and social talent, but which had been
> cultivated musically by a thorough technical training in
> the elegant and fastidious school of Mendelssohn, and
> by twenty years' work in composing for the drawing
> room, the church, the festival, and the concert room.
> . . . When he plunged into the banalities and trivialities
> of Savoy Opera he carried his old training with him
> . . . and his workmanship was unfailingly skilful and
> refined, even when the material was of the cheapest.[2]

The last remark sums up Shaw's attitude to Gilbert. His
antagonism began in 1894 when William Archer compared
the style of *Arms and the Man* to Gilbertian comedy.
Archer said that Shaw's characters, like Gilbert's, 'turn
their moral garments inside out and go about with the
linings displayed, flaunting the seams and raw edges and

stiffenings and paddings'.[3] Shaw accepted that both he and Gilbert demolished conventional ideals by exposing real motives and feelings, but he thought that Gilbert was merely a 'paradoxically humorous cynic' who – unlike Shaw – had no positive philosophy to substitute for destroyed ideals. He denied that Gilbert was in any way a serious dramatist, and thought the ideas in the operas were simply jokes:

> The theme of *The Pirates of Penzance* is essentially the same as that of Ibsen's *Wild Duck*; but we all understood that the joke of the pirate being the 'slave of duty' lay in the utter absurdity and topsyturviness of such a proposition, whereas when we read *The Wild Duck* we see that the exhibition of the same sort of slave there is no joke at all, but a grimly serious attack on our notion that we need stick at nothing in the cause of duty.[4]

Shaw's lifelong disparagement of him is surprising in view of his obvious indebtedness to Gilbert. From a historical vantage, the importance of the Savoy Operas in the development of modern British drama cannot be overlooked. They are the focal point of a transition phase in theatre which began with the production of Robertson's plays at the Prince of Wales' Theatre in the 1860s and ended with the English dramatic renaissance of the 1890s. During this period, the educated and moneyed upper and middle classes who had shunned the playhouses during the early part of Victoria's reign returned to the theatre. Increasingly, these classes discovered they could visit a theatre without offence or embarrassment. In the physical surroundings supplied first by the Bancrofts and later by D'Oyly Carte, they watched plays in comfort and security.

They saw that the theatre could provide a reflection – albeit sometimes a satiric one – of their own concerns and aspirations.

Gilbert was at the forefront of dramatists writing with this new highly educated audience in mind. Like the members of his audience, Gilbert had a university and professional training, and his operas are full of references and allusions comprehensible only to persons of similar educational background. A good example is the Major-General's song in *Pirates* which has a profusion of classical and historical references that would tax the knowledge of any modern student:

> I know our mythic history, King Arthur's and Sir Caradoc's,
> I answer hard acrostics, I've a pretty taste for paradox.
> I quote in elegiacs all the crimes of Heliogabalus,
> In conics I can floor peculiarities parabolous.
> I can tell undoubted Raphaels from Gerard Dows and Zoffanies,
> I know the croaking chorus from the *Frogs* of Aristophanes.

Sullivan's scores are just as scholarly in their parodic references to other composers. The Mikado's song, for example, contains a deft quotation from Bach at the point where the Mikado sings of 'masses and fugues and "ops"/By Bach, interwoven/With Spohr and Beethoven,/At Classical Monday Pops.'

The intellectual cleverness of the Savoy Operas signalled the restoration of wit as the dominant form of stage comedy after an absence of almost a century. The overall quality of their construction stimulated a new regard for playwriting as a respectable form of literary endeavour (Gilbert was the first British writer to receive a knighthood solely for his plays). In 1916, William Archer identified an important contribution by Gilbert to the development of modern drama. In his 1873 article on how to write a play, Gilbert advised that the first step should be the selection of a 'general idea' or theme. Archer was struck by the originality of the suggestion:

> It is noteworthy . . . and even a little surprising, that he starts from the assumption that a play should have a 'general idea', a theme, or, as we should say, a problem. There he was distinctly in advance of his time. His contemporaries, as a rule, thought of nothing but the telling of a perfectly trivial story, comic or sentimental, with no more social or spiritual relevance than may be found in the legend of Mother Hubbard.[5]

As a rule, the Savoy Operas are regarded as 'perfectly trivial', but close inspection shows the remarkable thematic unity that underlies their superficial fun and frivolity. This unity is best appreciated in the early operas, each of which is built around a 'general idea' which is the basis of plot and characterisation. *Pinafore* is a debate on the topic of human equality; *Pirates* is a burlesque morality play which attacks moral idealism. In his monograph on Gilbert, Max Sutton has written an eloquent summary of the thematic unity of *Iolanthe* in which he points out the fugue-like repetition of the theme of law. The central tension of the opera is created through the opposition of fairy law and mortal law; this conflict is expressed in the two settings (An Arcadian Landscape and Westminster) and is embodied in the character of Strephon, who is half-mortal and half-fairy. Sutton calls *Iolanthe* a 'drama of choice' because all the characters are faced with the dilemma of following their natural impulses or obeying the law. Iolanthe defies mortal law by marrying a mortal, and Strephon defies mortal law by marrying Phyllis. The leaders of the two camps, the Lord Chancellor and the Fairy Queen, struggle with feelings that conflict with their official duties: the Lord Chancellor loves Phyllis but is her guardian, and the Fairy Queen is attracted to Private Willis, a guardsman. At the end of the opera, the seriousness with which the characters have regarded the law is overthrown when the Lord Chancellor changes the law preventing fairies from marrying mortals by altering a single word. This solution 'invites everyone to view legal systems not as absolute powers but as arbitrary creations of man'.[6] A similar overturning of the law occurs at the end of *Pinafore*, *The Mikado* and *Ruddigore*.

The thematic unity of the Savoy Operas prefigures the 'drama of ideas' of Shaw where political and philosophical ideas are worked out through embodiment in various characters. Shaw's irritability at the notion that Gilbert was in any way a serious dramatist suggests that he secretly recognised and envied the originality of his predecessor. Indeed, Shaw's own plays, which began with the Ibsenite realism of *Widowers' Houses* (1892) and *Mrs. Warren's Profession* (1893) became increasingly Gilbertian in tone and technique. In *Shaw and the Nineteenth-Century Theatre*, Martin Meisel demonstrates Shaw's indebtedness to Gilbert:

> one can observe a clear movement from the Unpleasant Plays, with their contemporary middle-class settings, social concerns, and journalistic associations, to the late Extravaganzas, with their remote and fanciful settings, universal concerns, and associations with fairy tale, fable, and parable.[7]

Many of Shaw's later non-realistic plays are based on one of Gilbert's favourite devices, the 'interpenetration of the ordinary world and an imaginative otherworld' (p. 392). This device occurs repeatedly in the operas, from *The Sorcerer* where magic intrudes on a Victorian wedding to *Utopia* where a South Sea kingdom is disrupted by the arrival of English civilisation. Four of the five parts of Shaw's *Back to Methuselah* (1918–20) are set in Gilbertian 'otherworlds' which range from the past (B.C. 4004) to the future (A.D. 2170) and include such topsy-turvy Gilbertian ideas as the replacement of the entire British civil service by Chinese. Similar fantasy is found in Shaw's *The Apple Cart* (1929), *Too True to be Good* (1931) and *The Simpleton of the Unexpected Isles* (1934).

Meisel regards Shaw's return to Gilbertianism as a 'liberation from literal realism' of late-nineteenth-century drama. To the extent that he was never trapped by 'literal realism', Gilbert was ahead of his time. The free admixture of fantasy and reality in his plays and operas foreshadows not only the late plays of Shaw but also the plays of Pirandello and Ionesco. The philosophical outlook of Gilbert's drama also prefigures twentieth-century drama. Shaw was right when he said that Gilbert did not have a plan for the world; however, he did have a unified vision of human civilisation. In his plays and opera, Gilbert depicts human life as an endless conflict between arbitrary laws and the individual's true feelings and impulses. These laws may be fictional – as in *The Mikado* – or real – as in *The Sorcerer* – but they always impose restrictions on the characters' freedom of action. These arbitrary laws exist in a universe whose operation is unpredictable, illogical and governed by chance. In *Pinafore*, Sir Joseph tells Captain Corcoran not to patronise his crew because 'an accident of birth has placed you above them and them below you'. 'Accidents of birth' are a dominant feature of the operas. Frederic, whose birthday fell in leap year, is the prototype of a character whose life is governed by an event over which he had no control; other examples are Sir Despard Murgatroyd in *Ruddigore* who unwittingly inherited the baronetcy of Ruddigore and its attendant curse, and Marco and Giuseppe, one of whom is the king of Barataria and has been wed in infancy to Casilda. The characters feel quite rightly that their destiny is outside their control. Lurking beneath the events of the operas is fate, as Don Alhambra reminds us:

> Submit to Fate without unseemly wrangle;
>   Such complications frequently occur –
> Life is one closely complicated tangle:
>   Death is the only true unraveller!

This awareness of the unpredictability of human life leads to an undertone of pessimism and despair which occasionally percolates to the surface of the operas. In *Utopia*, King Paramount observes 'what a farce life is, to be sure', and then sings a grimly sardonic song which is the Gilbertian equivalent of Shakespeare's 'seven ages of man':

> First you're born – and I'll be bound you
> Find a dozen strangers round you.
> 'Hallo', cries the new-born baby,
> 'Where's my parents? Which may they be?'
>   Awkward silence – no reply –
>   Puzzled baby wonders why!
> Father rises, bows politely –
> Mother smiles (but not too brightly) –

Finale: Assessment

Doctor mumbles like a dumb thing –
Nurse is busy mixing something –
    Every symptom seems to show
    You're decidedly *de trop* –
Ho! ho! ho! ho! ho! ho! ho! ho!
    Time's teetotum
      If you spin it,
    Gives its quotum
      Once a minute
    I'll go bail
    You hit the nail,
    And you fail
      The deuce is in it!

The song chronicles the individual's hapless progress through love, marriage, and parenthood, until –

    Comes at last the final stroke –
    Time has had its little joke!

The operas' continued appeal to modern audiences is based as much on this unsentimental view of human life as on their superficial attributes of song, joke and rhyme. At the same time, the music and comedy of the operas rescues them from despair by provoking pleasure which is made more intense by knowledge of its transience. The ultimate message of the Savoy Operas is expressed in *The Gondoliers*:

    Life's a pudding full of plums,
    Care's a canker that benumbs.
    Wherefore waste our elocution
    On impossible solution?

Gilbert and Sullivan

Life's a pleasant institution,
    Let us take it as it comes!
Set aside the dull enigma,
    We shall guess it all too soon;
Failure brings no kind of stigma –
Dance we to another tune!
        String the lyre and fill the cup,
        Lest on sorrow we should sup.
        String the lyre and fill the cup,
        Lest on sorrow we should sup.
Hop and skip to Fancy's fiddle,
Hands across and down the middle –
Life's perhaps the only riddle
    That we shrink from giving up!

Notes

1. Overture: the Collaboration

1. Comment by Henry Chorley, librettist of Sullivan's first (unfinished and unproduced) opera, *The Sapphire Necklace*; quoted in Jacobs, *Arthur Sullivan*, p. 27.
2. Robert Papperitz, a Leipzig music teacher, quoted in Temperley (ed.) *Athlone History of Music in Britain*, p. 18.
3. Letters by both Sullivan and Gilbert outlining their artistic points of view are quoted fully in Jacobs *Arthur Sullivan*, Ch 20, 29.
4. Interview in *Cassell's Saturday Journal*, 21 March 1894.

2. Curtain-Raiser: the Theatrical Background

1. Stedman, *Gilbert Before Sullivan*, p. 1; this book gives an excellent account of pre-Gilbert and Sullivan Victorian musical entertainment, and reprints the texts of six of Gilbert's early comic plays.
2. Watson, *Sheridan to Robertson*, p. 6; this book and Rowell's *Victorian Theatre* are two indispensable histories of Victorian theatre.
3. *Saturday Review*, 28 September 1868.
4. Watson, *Sheridan to Robertson*, p. 349.
5. Henry James's amusing comments on the playgoing habits of Victorians are reprinted in Rowell, *Victorian Dramatic Criticism*, pp. 193–4.

6. Quoted in Baily, *Gilbert and Sullivan Book*, p. 343; Brooke, Parker and Spurgeon were eminent clergymen.

7. Augustin Filon's *The English Stage: Being an Account of the Victorian Drama* (published in 1897) is an interesting review of Victorian drama from a French perspective.

8. Kragaur, *Orpheus in Paris*, p. 175; this volume and the book by Moss and Marvel, *Cancan and Barcarolle*, give a good account of the development of *opéra bouffe*.

9. Rees, *Thespis*, p. 58; this scholarly book describes the production of *Thespis* in 1871 and gives a definitive text of the opera.

10. For comparison of Gilbert and Offenbach, see Rees, *Thespis*, p. 72.

11. Gagey, *Ballad Opera*, p. 4; this book gives a detailed description of the origin and development of ballad opera.

12. Temperley, 'The English Romantic Opera', *Victorian Studies*, 9, 293–301 (March 1966); the comment on 'Christmas card doggerel' is from Michael Hurd's chapter on 'Opera 1835–1865' in Temperley (ed.), *The Athlone History of Music in Britain*, and the comment on the libretto of *The Sapphire Necklace* is from Sullivan and Flower, *Sir Arthur Sullivan*.

13. Filon, *English Stage*, p. 93; see also Appleton, *Madame Vestris*.

14. The opening night programme at the Gaiety is described in Mander and Mitcheson, *The Lost Theatres of London*; the quotation from *Robert the Devil* is from a text in the British Library (London: Phillips, no date).

3. The Masterpiece: 'The Mikado'

1. See Pendle, *Eugene Scribe and the French Opera of the Nineteenth Century*, for a thorough enumeration and analysis of Scribe's techniques.

2. The complete text of *Box and Cox* is in Booth (ed.), *English Plays: IV, Farces*.

3. Booth, 'Introduction', *English Plays: IV*, p. 31.

4. Frye, *Anatomy of Criticism*, pp. 163ff.

5. In *The Annotated Gilbert and Sullivan*, Ian Bradley explains 'Parliamentary trains' in this way: 'An Act of 1844 had compelled railway companies to run at least one train a day on all lines which stopped at every station with a fare of one penny a mile.' The slow speed of these trains gave rise to their name.

6. See David Daiches' analysis of Housman, Kipling, Hardy and other late Victorian writers in *Some Late Victorian Attitudes*.

7. Houghton, *The Victorian Frame of Mind*, p. 404; this book is essential for understanding the philosophical temper of the age.

Notes

4. A Victorian Looking-Glass: 'The Sorcerer' and 'H.M.S. Pinafore'

1. From *English Hours*, quoted in Best, *Mid-Victorian Britain 1851–75*, p. 270.
2. Altick, *Victorian People and Ideas*, p. 27; this book is a good introduction to the historical and social background of Victorian drama.
3. James Morris, *Heaven's Command* (London: Faber and Faber, 1973), p. 23; Morris' *Pax Britannica* trilogy is a useful background for the imperialist allusions in the Savoy Operas.
4. Booth, *Prefaces*, p. 27.
5. Quoted in Best, *Mid-Victorian Britain, 1851–75*, p. 255; Palmerston was British prime minister from 1855–8 and 1859–65.
6. James Froude, quoted in Houghton, *The Victorian Frame of Mind*, p. 187; this statement summarises the theme of many Victorian novels, especially those by Trollope and Dickens.
7. For a full discussion of Smiles' life and work, see Chapter 5 of Briggs' *Victorian People*.

5. Through the Looking-Glass: 'The Pirates of Penzance' and 'Patience'

1. Booth's *English Melodrama* is a full discussion of the themes and topics of melodrama.
2. See Houghton, *The Victorian Frame of Mind* and Best, *Mid-Victorian Britain 1851–75*, for detailed discussion of the Victorian moral code.
3. See Briggs, *Victorian People*, Chapter 5.
4. Houghton, *The Victorian Frame of Mind*, p. 280.
5. Altick, *Victorian People and Ideas*, p. 292; this book has a good overview of the aesthetic movement.
6. Houghton, *The Victorian Frame of Mind*, p. 410.
7. Vicinus' *Suffer and Be Still* describes the social and legal position of women in the nineteenth century.

6. Retreat from Satire: 'The Gondoliers'

1. Bradley reproduces this song and many other deleted numbers from the operas in his edition; they are found in the Lord Chamberlain's licence copy of the operas.
2. See Jacobs, *Arthur Sullivan*, pp. 186–7.
3. Thomson, *England in the Nineteenth Century*, p. 174.

4. The full diary entry is quoted in Bradley, vol. 1, p. 402.

5. Hicks' rather unpleasant memories of Gilbert are found in his autobiography, *Between Ourselves* (London: Cassell, 1930), pp. 49ff.

6. Concerning Gilbert's depiction of 'stout and mature ladies', Shaw said: 'Such fun has always revolted me; and I am waiting for the time when it will revolt the public too' (*Our Theatres in the Nineties*, I, p. 222).

7. Gilbert and Sullivan in Performance

1. Baily, *Book*, p. 425.

2. Quoted in Dark and Grey, *W. S. Gilbert*, p. 152.

3. Donaldson, *The Actor Managers*, p. 84.

4. Quoted in Baily, *Book*, p. 60.

5. From Lytton's autobiography, *A Wandering Minstrel* (1933).

6. Quoted in Dark and Grey, *W. S. Gilbert*, pp. 37ff.

7. Quoted in Baily, *Book*, p. 104.

8. Watson, *Sheridan to Robertson*, p. 339.

9. See Booth, 'The Acting of Charles Mathews', in *English Plays: IV*; this volume also reprints the text of *Patter Versus Clatter*.

10. The full text of this comic song as well as others by Grossmith is found in Tony Joseph's biography, *George Grossmith*.

11. These stage directions are taken from early libretti of *Trial*; they are reprinted in Bradley, vol. 2.

12. Peter Hall, *Peter Hall's Diaries* (London: Hamish Hamilton, 1983), p. 178.

13. Quiller-Couch, Arthur, 'W. S. Gilbert', p. 162, in Jones (ed.), *W. S. Gilbert*.

8. Finale: Assessment

1. Morris, *Heaven's Command*, p. 39.

2. Shaw, *Music in London*, I, pp. 226–7.

3. Rowell, *Victorian Dramatic Criticism*, p. 306.

4. Shaw, *Music in London*, I, p. 226.

5. Archer, William (ed.), *'A Stage Play' by W. S. Gilbert* (New York: reprinted by the theatre museum of Columbia University, 1916).

6. Sutton, *W. S. Gilbert*, p. 106.

7. Meisel, *Shaw and the Nineteenth-Century Theatre*, p. 380.

Bibliography

The Savoy Opera Libretti

Allen, Reginald (ed.), *The First Night Gilbert and Sullivan* (Chappell, 1975).

Bradley, Ian (ed.), *The Annotated Gilbert and Sullivan* (Penguin, 1982 vol. 1; 1984 vol. 2).

Green, Martyn (ed.), *Martyn Green's Treasury of Gilbert and Sullivan* (New York: Simon and Schuster, 1961).

Hudson, Derek (ed.), *The Savoy Operas* (Oxford University Press, 1963).

Plays and Poems by W. S. Gilbert

Ellis, James (ed.), *The Bab Ballads by W. S. Gilbert* (Cambridge, Mass.: Harvard University Press, 1970).

Rowell, George (ed.), *Plays by W. S. Gilbert* (Cambridge University Press, 1983).

Stedman, Jane (ed.), *Gilbert Before Sullivan: Six Comic Plays* (Chicago: Chicago University Press, 1967).

Reference Books

Ayre, Leslie, *The Gilbert and Sullivan Companion* (Pan Books, 1974).

Benford, Harry, *The Gilbert and Sullivan Lexicon* (New York: Richards Rosen, 1978).

Gilbert and Sullivan

Biography and Production History

Allen, Reginald, *Sir Arthur Sullivan* (New York: Pierpont Morgan Library, 1975).

Baily, Leslie, *Gilbert and Sullivan and their World* (Thames and Hudson, 1973).

Baily, Leslie, *The Gilbert and Sullivan Book* (Cassell, 1952; reissued Spring Books, 1966).

Cellier, Francois and Bridgeman, Cunningham, *Gilbert and Sullivan and their operas* (Pitman, 1914; reissued New York: Blom, 1970).

Dark, Sidney and Grey, Rowland, *W. S. Gilbert: His Life and Letters* (Methuen, 1923; reissued New York: Blom, 1972).

Jacobs, Arthur, *Arthur Sullivan: A Victorian Musician* (Oxford University Press, 1984).

Pearson, Hesketh, *Gilbert and Sullivan* (Hamish Hamilton, 1935; reissued Penguin Books, 1985).

Pearson, Hesketh, *Gilbert: His Life and Strife* (New York: Harper, 1957).

Sullivan, Herbert and Flower, Newman, *Sir Arthur Sullivan: His Life, Letters, and Diaries* (Cassell, 1927; reissued 1950).

Wilson, Robin and Lloyd, Frederic, *Gilbert and Sullivan: The D'Oyly Carte Years* (Weidenfeld and Nicolson, 1984).

Wolfson, John, *Final Curtain* (Chappell, 1976).

Young, Percy, *Sir Arthur Sullivan* (New York: Norton, 1971).

Criticism

Frye, Northrop, *The Anatomy of Criticism* (Princeton: Princeton University Press, 1957).

Helyar, James (ed.), *Gilbert and Sullivan: Papers presented at the International Conference held at the University of Kansas in May 1970* (Lawrence, Kansas: University of Kansas Libraries, 1971).

Jones, John Bush (ed.), *W. S. Gilbert: A Century of Scholarship and Commentary* (New York: New York University Press, 1970).

Sutton, Max Keith, *W. S. Gilbert* (Boston: Twayne, 1975).

Williamson, Audrey, *Gilbert and Sullivan Opera: An Assessment* (New York: Macmillan, 1953; Boston: Marion Boyars, 1982).

Theatrical Background

Appleton, W. W., *Madame Vestris and the London Stage* (New York: Columbia University Press, 1974).

Bibliography

Bailey, J. O., *British Plays of the Nineteenth Century* (New York: Odyssey, 1966).

Booth, Michael R., *English Melodrama* (H. Jenkin, 1965).

Booth, Michael R. (ed.), *English Plays of the Nineteenth Century: III. Comedies: IV. Farces* (Clarendon Press, 1973).

Booth, Michael R. (ed.), *The Magistrate and Other Nineteenth-Century Plays* (Oxford University Press, 1974).

Booth, Michael R., *Prefaces to English Nineteenth-Century Theatre* (Manchester University Press, 1980).

Donaldson, Frances, *The Actor-Managers* (Chicago: Henry Regnery, 1970).

Gagey, Edmond M., *Ballad Opera* (New York: Blom, 1965).

Howard, Diana, *London Theatres and Music-Halls 1850–1950* (Library Association, 1970).

Joseph, Tony, *George Grossmith* (published by the author, 1982).

Kragaur, Siegfried, *Orpheus in Paris: Offenbach and the Paris of his Time* (New York: Vienna House, 1972).

Laurence, Dan A. (ed.), *Bernard Shaw: Collected Letters 1874–1897* (New York: Dodd, Mead, 1965).

Mander, Raymond and Mitchenson, Joe, *The Lost Theatres of London* (New York: Taplinger, 1968).

Mayer, David, *Harlequin in his Element* (Cambridge, Mass.: Cambridge University Press, 1969).

Meisel, Martin, *Shaw and the Nineteenth-Century Theatre* (Princeton: Princeton University Press, 1963).

Moss, Arthur and Marvel, Evalyn, *Cancan and Barcarolle: The Life and Times of Jacques Offenbach* (Westport, Conn.: Greenwood Press, 1975).

Nicoll, Allardyce, *A History of Late Nineteenth-Century Drama* (Cambridge University Press, 1949).

Pendle, Karin, *Eugene Scribe and the French Opera of the Nineteenth Century* (Ann Arbor: University Microfilms International, 1979).

Rees, Terence, *Thespis: A Gilbert and Sullivan Enigma* (Dillon's University Bookshop, 1964).

Rowell, George (ed.), *Nineteenth Century Plays* (Oxford University Press, 1972).

Rowell, George (ed.), *Victorian Dramatic Criticism* (Methuen, 1971).

Rowell, George, *The Victorian Theatre* (Clarendon Press, 1967).

Shaw, George Bernard, *Our Theatres in the Nineties* (Constable, 1935).

Shaw, George Bernard, *Music in London* (Constable, 1935).

Stokes, John, *Resistible Theatres: Enterprise and experiment in the late nineteenth-century theatre* (Paul Elek, 1972).

Taylor, John Russell, *The Rise and Fall of the Well-Made Play* (New York: Hill and Wang, 1967).

Temperley, Nicholas (ed.), *The Athlone History of Music in Britain. Volume V: The Romantic Age* (The Athlone Press, 1981).

Watson, Ernest B., *Sheridan to Robertson: A Study of the Nineteenth-Century London Stage* (New York: Blom, 1963).

White, Eric Walter, *The Rise of English Opera* (New York: Philosophical Library, 1951).

Historical and Cultural Background

Altick, Richard D., *Victorian People and Ideas* (Dent, 1973).

Best, Geoffrey, *Mid-Victorian Britain 1851–75* (Weidenfeld and Nicholson, 1971).

Briggs, Asa, *Victorian People* (New York: Harper and Row, 1955).

Daiches, David, *Some Late Victorian Attitudes* (Andre Deutsch, 1969).

Houghton, Walter, *The Victorian Frame of Mind* (Oxford University Press, 1957).

Martin, Robert B., *The Triumph of Wit: A Study of Victorian Comic Theory* (Clarendon Press, 1974).

Thomson, David, *England in the Nineteenth Century* (Penguin Books, 1950; reissued 1983).

Vicinus, Martha (ed.), *Suffer and Be Still: Women in the Victorian Age* (Bloomington: Indiana University Press, 1972).

Index

183

Index

Index

186